TLC
LIFE UNSCRIPTED

THE CARS OF
OVERHAULIN'
WITH CHIP FOOSE

DAIN GINGERELLI

MOTORBOOKS

First published in 2007 by Motorbooks, an imprint of MBI Publishing Company, Galtier Plaza, Suite 200, 380 Jackson Street, St. Paul, MN 55101-3885 USA

MBI Publishing Company titles are also available at discounts in bulk quantity for industrial or sales-promotional use. For details write to Special Sales Manager at MBI Publishing Company, Galtier Plaza, Suite 200, 380 Jackson Street, St. Paul, MN 55101-3885 USA

©2007 Discovery Communications, Inc. TLC, *Overhaulin'* and associed logos are trademarks of Discovery Communications, Inc. used under license. All rights reserved.
tlc.discovery.com/overhaulin

Discovery Communications
Book Development Team:
David Abraham, EVP & General Manager, TLG
Carol LeBlanc, VP, Licensing
Elizabeth Bakacs, VP, Creative Services
Caitlin Erb, Licensing Specialist

ISBN-13: 978-0-7603-2412-7
ISBN-10: 0-7603-2412-3

Editors: Jennifer Bennett and Zack Miller
Designer: Rochelle Brancato and Sara Holle

Printed in China

Library of Congress Cataloging-in-Publication Data

Gingerelli, Dain, 1949-
  The cars of *Overhaulin'* with Chip Foose / Dain Gingerelli.
    p. cm.
  ISBN-13: 978-0-7603-2412-7 (softbound)
  ISBN-10: 0-7603-2412-3 (softbound)
  1. Automobiles--Customizing. 2. Automobiles--Conservation and restoration. 3. Automobiles--Maintenance and repair. I. Foose, Chip. II. *Overhaulin'* (TV show) III. Title.
  TL255.2.G55 2007
  629.28'72--dc22
                        2006017045

On the cover:
(Main) *Bad brakes and a loud exhaust system earmarked John Parks' pride and joy, a 1952 GMC pickup truck, for a truly wild overhaul. John had already put some time and work into customizing his ride, but it was nothing compared to what the Overhaulin' team was about to do—all in seven days. Starting with a new crate engine from Guaranty Chevrolet, the build only got better. D&P Classic and No Limit Engineering overhauled the suspension, Diff Works gave it a new rear end, Caliber Collision repaired and painted the body, and Alphasonik installed the sound system.*

(Back Cover) *Chip Foose and the A-Team tackle another project for their weekly television program Overhaulin'. Each week another unsuspecting car owner is targeted to have his or her car completely overhauled by the team. And when each car and truck is finished, and returned to its owner, chances are good that you'll find a new and unique set of Foose Design wheels on it.*

On the titlepage: *A car's not officially considered overhauled until new wheels are mounted—in this case they came from Foose Design.*

CONTENTS

ACKNOWLEDGMENTS

Just as the cars of *Overhaulin'* represent the collective work by the A-Team, this book is the culmination of a team effort. It was my job as the book's author to condense into a given number of pages the stories behind each car. But my work would have been much more difficult without the cooperation and support of a small cadre of people associated with the show.

The group effort began in St. Paul, Minnesota, where MBI Publishing's editorial staff decided to go ahead with a book about Chip Foose's popular television program. After more than a few phone conversations and e-mails with editorial director Zack Miller, we decided that the book had merit. Thank you, Zack, for entrusting me with the project, and thanks also to Carson Lev, Chip's marketing manager and confidant, for briefing me on the goals as set forth by Foose Design.

I would be remiss if I didn't, at this time, mention two key players to this project—Cynthia Whorton and Jennifer Bennett. Cynthia served as my immediate contact at Brentwood Productions, sacrificing valuable office time to chase down photographs of the subject cars, and making sure that I had the right information about the A-Team members, marks, insiders, and accomplices to complete each chapter. Her efforts are much appreciated by this humble writer. As my editor, Jennifer spent many long hours making sure that the copy reads smoothly, and generally watching my p's and q's. One thing I learned early in my career is that good research background and editing is essential to a successful writer. Thank you, Cynthia and Jennifer.

Two other women instrumental in the completion of this book are Chip's office manager at Foose Design, Lynne Stout, and the show's supervising producer, Veronica Torres. Like master sergeants in the army, Lynne and Veronica make things happen on time. Want to know the whereabouts of Chip Foose? Check with Lynne. Need to know the status of the next overhaul? Veronica can tell you.

Obviously, the book never would have gone to print if the program *Overhaulin'* hadn't been conceived by Bud Brutsman. This young producer has established himself as a visionary in the business, and clearly this particular reality TV series casts him at the forefront of Hollywood's young creatives. Bud is a bundle of energy, too, perhaps equaled only by Chip Foose himself. And let's not forget about the network that brought *Overhaulin'* to viewers: TLC. Thanks so much for airing such a great program.

I also want to take this moment to pay tribute to the Marks, Insiders, and Accomplices who appeared on the program and who are featured in this book. Without their enthusiasm and willingness to play along with the pranks (or be pranked), the program would never have grabbed the public's attention so successfully. Nor could this book touch the human element so deeply.

Ditto for the suppliers and parts vendors who assist with each overhaul. As a car guy, I know how costly it can be to rebuild a car to the level that the A-Team strives for with each build; having the proper tools and parts is essential. I salute you all.

It takes more than words, though, to acknowledge the contributions made by Chip Foose and the A-Team. Again, speaking as a car guy, I can appreciate their talents and love for this hobby, but as an author and fan of *Overhaulin'*, I can't even begin to fathom the amount of work, time, and energy they put into each project. I doff my shop hat to them. They are people I admire, if not envy.

I give special thanks to my wife, Donna, and our teenage boys, Kyle and Chris, too, for sacrificing Gingerelli family time together so that I could complete this project. Thank you, too, for sharing a few evenings of your time with me while we watched various episodes. "Research" is a valuable tool for a writer.

Finally, I thank the Big Shop Foreman for giving me the opportunity to make my living as an automotive writer, working with people in a business that I truly enjoy. For as the *Overhaulin'* theme song states: "I love gasoline."

Dain Gingerelli
Mission Viejo, California
May 2006

INTRODUCTION

Chip Foose

I'm just as passionate about cars as I am design, and combining these passions is what drives the projects in my life. Whether I'm designing, building, repairing, driving, or even overhauling, there's nothing I enjoy on this earth more—other than my friends and family—than cars. It's been that way practically my entire life, too. Ever since my dad, Sam Foose, showed me the way around his garage when I was a boy, my life has centered around automobiles. And I've loved every minute, hour, and day spent in the garage working on cars, whether they belong to me or somebody else. That time spent includes those long, challenging days shared with the

Overhaulin' A-Team to rebuild cars that, for the most part, belong to complete strangers.

But the truth is, even though the A-Team and I don't personally know the car owners—the Mark as we call them on the program—when we begin each overhaul, by the end of the week we feel that we know that person intimately. That's because on *Overhaulin'* we do more than just rebuild cars. We build relationships. As I've said many times before, *Overhaulin'* is not just about the cars. It's about the people—in this case the individuals who own the cars that we overhaul. And I think it's building those relationships, more than anything else, that has established *Overhaulin'* as one of the

favorite automotive reality shows on television today.

The A-Team and I have a lot of fun on the set during the overhauls, too. Don't get me wrong, everybody on the A-Team, along with the supporting vendors and suppliers who go out of their way to make sure we have all the right tools, parts, and components to complete the build, work hard to finish each car. Let me rephrase that: we work hard to finish the Mark's *dream* car, because that is the underlying theme of *Overhaulin'*—to complete project cars for people who don't otherwise have the time, resources, or perhaps abilities to make their dream ride a reality.

That's what I love and respect most about A-Team members: their unselfish devotion to our mission. With each overhaul, I surround myself with some of the most talented and enthusiastic fabricators, painters, engine builders, upholsterers, and craftsmen—and craftswomen—in the automotive world. I'm proud to share the same shop with these people for a week as we transform cars that amount to what *Overhaulin'* cohost Chris Jacobs often describes as "a bucket of bolts" into custom vehicles that any diehard enthusiast would appreciate and love to be seen in.

Each project car is special in its own right. Many of the cars had been—before the overhaul even began—passed along from one family member to another. As you might imagine, these vehicles are even

Chip Foose taking time out in one of his favorite overhauls— Wyo Tech's 1956 Chevrolet "Speedster."

more special to their current owners, so when a car rolls into the shop for the A-Team to begin its overhaul, we treat that set of wheels as though it were our own restoration project, our own hand-me-down. In the process, we create a family heirloom, a custom car or truck that reflects the personality and passion of its owner such that every time a family member gets behind the steering wheel and turns the ignition key, they're turning another page in the family album. Like I said, it's about building personal relationships.

Even though I feel that *Overhaulin'* is as much about the people as the cars we build, I'm constantly asked which of the overhauled cars is my favorite. And while I might reply, "The

next one," I will confess that certain episodes are especially memorable to me. In terms of builds, I take special pride in how the A-Team converted WyoTech's all-original 1956 Chevrolet Bel Air four-door sedan into a show-stopping two-door speedster. In fact, many of the A-Team members for that episode happened to be faculty members, students, or alumni from that famous trade-tech institute in Laramie, Wyoming.

I also take pride in the episode known as "Search & Rescue." That overhaul involved a 1988 Chevy pickup belonging to a high school honor student who was also a junior firefighter. A conversion job like that would normally take two or three months, but like every overhaul per-

It's all smiles for the camera as Chip gets into his disguise.

In addition to seven Tour de France wins, Lance Armstrong has one overhaul.

formed by the A-Team, we did it in a week's time.

Same for the 1977 El Camino that we overhauled for the episode "Surfer Kid." The cameras didn't even begin to show the work that we put into the tonneau cover and surfboard racks. And nobody would have done what we did to the 1950 Ford in "Museum Worthy." There's a lot of interesting sheet-metal work in that car, and even though time didn't allow all the fabrication work to be shown when the episode aired, the A-Team took personal pride in their work, because for them, the real reward is found in the Mark's expression during the reveal on Day 7.

That brings up another interesting point about our show. Why did we

select seven days as the time period for an overhaul? Why not a month, or two days, or simply follow along for a season while we built a show-winning custom? Simple: I felt that a select group of fabricators and builders could complete an overhaul in a week's time. I based this theory on my experience working with my dad when I was a young man. He and I restored many of our customers' cars in two or three weeks' time. If two men could do it in that time span, I figured a team of select workers could accomplish the same feat in a week's time. I'm proud to say that, with one exception so far, we've always met our deadline. That exception was a Model A two door that had previously been semi-converted into a phaeton, or tub,

Overhaulin' is more than about rebuilding cars—it's about building relationships, too.

as hot rodders call them. The A-Team had to finish some of that conversion before we could continue, and then with the deadline approaching fast, I asked them to go an extra mile to give the car a coat of gloss black paint, rather than the primer that we had originally decided on. The extra time required for the paint to dry put us over the deadline, but I'll stand by my decision because the car turned out exceptionally nice.

Whether or not we miss another deadline, though, is incidental. The real impact that *Overhaulin'* has had on the automotive industry is immeasurable because we've bridged a gap between people who feel that their dream cars are unattainable, and giving them completed cars rep-

resenting the upper echelon of what dream rides are really all about.

And as A-Team members will tell you, a dream ride is as much about the people who build and drive the car as the car itself. In short, it's about the overhaul.

I hope you enjoy this book as much as we enjoyed creating the cars and trucks that are featured on its pages. We've featured a handful of the overhauled cars built during the show's first three seasons, and as you'll read, each episode has its own unique story behind it. And it's those unique stories that have helped fuel my passion for cars for so many years as a custom-car enthusiast.

'50 FORD
Chuck De Heras

Chuck
De Heras

Chuck De Heras grew up a hot rodder in
Southern California. He bought his first car,
a 1956 Buick, while attending Glendale High
School in 1959. Two years later he rebuilt the
Buick to a level that it won a fair share of
custom car show trophies. Most recently his
cars have appeared in the granddaddy of
custom car shows, the Grand National
Roadster Show, and on the covers of national
street rod magazines.

Experience tells us that museum docents and curators are forthright, honest people. We trust them, much as we do librarians, nurses, and school crosswalk guards. They help form the cornerstones of our society, and we seldom question their integrity.

So Chuck De Heras, who owns a small stable of hot rods, didn't give it a second thought when Dick Messer asked to borrow his stock 1950 Ford Coupe for a brief period. Messer is not only one of Chuck's friends and confidants, he also happens to be director of the renowned Petersen Automotive Museum in Los Angeles, a position that also made him the perfect choice as an accomplice on the third episode of TLC's *Overhaulin'*. Chuck obliged Dick's request to use the Ford for a museum exhibit, and with the help of his son, Derek, Chuck delivered the black Ford to the Petersen Museum, no questions asked. The sting was on, and when it was over the episode qualified as a museum piece in itself.

Derek De Heras

"My dad has been the biggest influence in my life, and hot rods have given us a common interest and hobby to share together," says Derek De Heras, who shows his gratitude for his father's help in getting his own 1932 Ford Roadster back on the road. It was payback time, and Derek was ready to help the A-Team with the 1950 Ford's rebuild. "*Overhaulin'* his '50 Ford is the perfect way to show him my appreciation," adds Derek. That they stung Chuck in the process, well, maybe that helped make up for some of those spankings Derek received while growing up!

Dave Messer

If Dave Messer resigns from his position as director of the Petersen Automotive Museum, he can drive a few miles down the road to Hollywood to work as an actor. His performance as the accomplice for episode three made him, in the words of co-host Chris Jacobs, "an actor for the ages." Dick played the fall guy, right down to being handcuffed by police officers for the final act, convincing Chuck once and for all that his car had been stolen—by Dick himself!

Chuck De Heras loaned his 1950 Ford to the Petersen Automotive Museum thinking it was to be used for an exhibit, not realizing that the A-Team was to use it as Exhibit A for an Overhaulin' *episode.*

At one point, the Ford Coupe had its interior refurbished with new upholstery on the seats and door panels. The classic large-diameter steering wheel had been wrapped with leather, too.

It was one thing to sucker-punch Chuck into delivering the car to the museum, but getting him to bite the bait so he believed the car had then been stolen from the museum was another task. That's where *Overhaulin'* co-hosts Chris Jacobs and Courtney Hansen, working with Dick Messer, came into play—because it required some fine acting by all three to convince Chuck that his car was now in the hands of thieves, not the reputable Petersen Automotive Museum.

In truth, while Chris and Courtney—acting as insurance claims adjustors—and Dick conducted their first meeting with Chuck in a conference room on the museum's fourth floor to discuss the car's disappearance, the Ford was being plucked apart in the museum's basement by *Overhaulin'*s A-Team. By the end of Day 1, the all-original Ford Coupe was in pieces, its vital organs spread out on the concrete floor for all to see, well, everybody but Chuck.

A major factor in Chuck's decision to buy the Ford for restoration was because its body was so straight and clean.

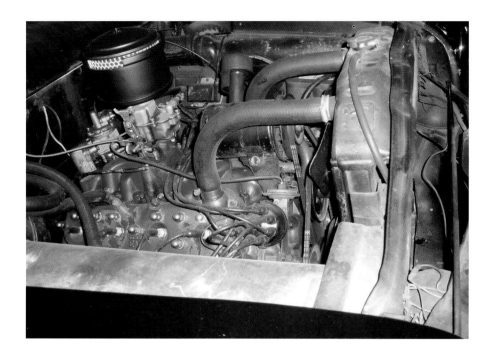

The flathead was Ford's first V-8 design, originally introduced in 1932. By 1950, it was long in the tooth, but today it's considered a classic worth keeping, which the A-Team did.

Indeed, within seven days, Chuck's customized Ford's pedigree would boast some legendary names on its build sheet. Helping Chip Foose with the overhaul was Troy Trepanier, who has built some of the top customs in the country, and Pete Eastwood, a man instrumental in putting hundreds of hot rods and old-car restorations back on the road. Chip and Troy brought top metal fabricators Bryan Fuller and Jared Zimmerman to the team, and Jim Griffin was called in to stitch the Ford's new interior. Mitch Lanzini applied the paint, which included a mix dubbed Grand Theft Green, and Chip designed the flashy wheels exclusively for this project.

Despite the A-Team's credentials, at one point during the overhaul Chip confessed to the camera that creating a custom car in a week's time can be a

Those two chromed stereo speaker covers were popular back in the 1960s. While the Ford's upholstery and interior trim were in decent condition, some of its components reveal how old the car is.

monumental task. "The most difficult part in designing a car and doing things is you don't know if it's right or wrong until you do it," he said. Those words were spoken around the time Jared, Bryan, and Pete were busy welding, hammering, and grinding on the 55-year-old sheet metal, so there was no turning back. And while Chuck believed that his car really had been stolen, there was no stealing time so the A-Team could take a breather.

Meanwhile, Chuck, convinced that his car was gone forever, bought another '50 Ford. He also figured that he could partially finance the new purchase by selling whatever parts would be recovered from the stolen car. In reference to the replacement car and how it compared to the overhauled coupe, A-Team member Jared said to the

After selecting a color scheme that reflected the art deco era, Chip Foose and the crew rolled the car to Mitch Lanzini's paint shop where the two-tone colors were applied.

camera: "The sad part is, this thing's probably going to be better than anything he bought."

And it was, but perhaps just as worthy was Dick Messer's final performance during the reveal on Day 7. That's when Chuck learned that Dick had "stolen" the car himself, and while the museum's director stood handcuffed before Chuck, the finished car sat only a few feet away, safe inside the museum, where it awaited its rightful owner.

Mission accomplished. Chuck had bought the grand-theft story from beginning to end. And when the ruse was revealed, he asked members of the A-Team to autograph the engine bay. "This is a piece of art. These guys are artists," he said. But in the end, there's no denying that it was the car that stole the show.

17

'77 EL CAMINO
Mylan Hayes

Mylan Hayes

Mylan has been surfing most of his life, and when he was 13 years old he saved a woman from drowning in a rip current. He refers to the '77 El Camino as "my baby." His stepfather handed over the keys to Mylan when he turned 17, and from that point on the aging Chevrolet became the official surfmobile. Little did Mylan know that day when he waved bye-bye to the car as it was towed away that only one week later he'd end up with a set of wheels that would make him the envy of Surf City.

Here's the deal: You're 19 years old, you're a business major in college who's footloose and fancy free with the rest of your adult life untapped and waiting. Moreover, you live at home with your parents in Huntington Beach, California, considered the surfing capital of the West Coast by many beachgoers. And that's a good thing, because you're also a surfer who likes to take to the water every morning. You and your board get to the beach thanks to your trusty '77 El Camino that your stepdad gave you a couple of years ago. Life is good.

That's the good news. The bad news is that A) The El Camino has a few—OK, about a gazillion—mechanical problems. B) There's still that matter of a citation for a broken seat belt that's unresolved and constantly looming over your head. And, C) '77 El Caminos are anything but attractive, something you're about to learn because Chip Foose & Company are about to overhaul your car, and you won't find out until seven days after you lose the car when

Tom and Vicki Slyman

Mylan has a close bond with his mother and stepdad, which made the sting easier for the A-Team, but perhaps a little difficult for Mom and Dad. During the overhaul, Tom recounted how Mylan responded to his car being towed away: "He always tries to maintain an upbeat and positive attitude. He was real excited, with nervous energy because he didn't know why it [the car] was taken." Tom's final words for the camera before Mylan was presented with his overhauled ride: "Mylan, you've been overhauled."

For serious surfers, the car's interior doubles as a locker room for street clothes. The cab for Mylan's '77 El Camino was no different.

it's "accidentally" towed away by the city. In the meantime, Chip's prognosis for the targeted El Camino is this: "We're working with something that doesn't have good bones to start with." In layman's terms, the '77 El Camino is, well, ugly.

The Mark in this case is one young Mylan Hayes, and while he was giving a surf lesson one morning to none other that Tod Schellinger (whose day job was producer for *Overhaulin'*), his black El Camino got towed away only moments before he could react. Never to give up, Mylan tried desperately to chase down the tow truck. Oh, how he tried, but to no avail. The conspiracy was on, and it only got better when Mylan's mother, Vicki, brought her son to

The point of no return. The deconstruction process is practically complete, and now the fun—and work—begins. The front grille shell is from a Monte Carlo.

the impound yard where the car was "held" until they could pay the bail to get it out. Enter the bad guy—Chris Jacobs in the guise of the tow-truck operator—who jostled and toyed with Mylan's emotions, in the process revealing that in order to free the car the registered owner—one Tom Slyman, Mylan's stepfather—would have to hand over $1,200 and sign for the car.

Life was no longer fun for surfer-dude Mylan, and it got only worse as

A lot of work went into transforming the El Camino's body work. Here Chip Foose reworks the rear bumper.

When the engine—considered the heartbeat of any cool car—is lowered into the engine bay, the mood in the shop lightens as the end of the project draws near.

Part of the Overhaulin' *magic included fabricating a new hood from scratch. Everybody pitched in to do their share so the overhaul was completed in a week.*

the week progressed, for without his wheels he couldn't get his board to the beach. Little did Mylan know that only a couple miles away at Stitchcraft Interiors' shop his car was being overhauled by some of the top fabricators and car builders in the country. As a bonus, Tyler Hatzikian, who forms surfboards for a living and owns Tyler Surf, custom-built a couple of new surfboards to match the finished car.

And what a car the A-Team was overhaulin' for Mylan! The ugly black paint was stripped, a more stylish Monte Carlo front grille was grafted to the reconditioned sheet

While Chip is considered a master fabricator, he's also a gifted artist. He creates an artist's rendering for each Overhaulin' *project before work begins.*

Chip wanted the graphics to reflect Mylan's personality and lifestyle, so he sketched what appears to be crashing waves on the side of the car's bed.

metal, and they created a zippy custom hood, using two existing ones—no small feat in itself—to set this Camino apart from all others. Viewers also got a lesson in how body paint graphics come together when Chip laid out side murals that resembled breaking waves on the ocean.

"I try to piece together something that matches the person's personality or lifestyle," said Chip. And for Mylan, this meant surfing. Watching Pete Santini's paint crew make the graphics come to life was nothing short of brilliant.

Ah, but surfing is more than just a visual experience. It's about the sounds of the waves crashing on shore and the rhythm of your own heartbeat as you catch what, for the

Running behind schedule, Chip enlisted the help of talented veteran pinstriper Dennis Rickliffs to assist with the graphics.

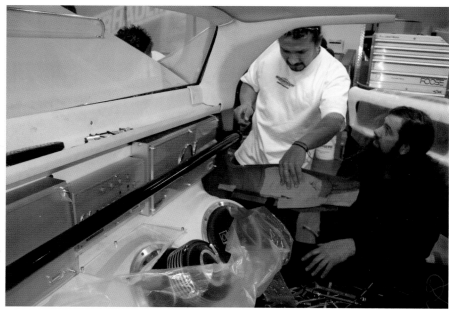

Revo (Stitchcrafters Interiors) and Ricky Anderson (Aphasonik) work to set the sound system in place before the upholstery is applied and stitched.

moment, is the perfect wave. To add that aspect to the design, the A-Team called on Alphasonik for a full line of audio gear (amps, processors, subwoofers and speakers, and accompanying components powerful enough to rattle dentures) to place beneath the Stitchcraft Interiors upholstery that was applied by Revo and his crew. The interior was a work of art in itself, too, with all seat sections cut using CAD programs for a precise fit.

Moving to the engine compartment of Mylan's car revealed a rather worn-out smog-control-choked mill. According to stepdad Tom, a valve job

A locker room no more! Form-fitting bucket seats with four-point belts, a custom steering wheel, and a sound system that will curl your toes make sure of that.

Mylan's "baby" looks like the A-Team gave it more than just a little TLC. Who would have thought that just seven days before it was a tired old car?

had been performed at about 80,000 miles, and by now the odometer read 150,000 and counting. So the A-Team gave the tired small block the "Chip" shot, replacing it with a new crate motor—a 350 V-8 from Guaranty Chevrolet. Foose Design wheels sit at each corner, this time wrapped with stylish BFGoodrich rubber.

When the car was ready, Mylan was brought in and teased some more before the reveal. Taken aback, all he could say was, "Thank you, oh, thank you," to each person on the A-Team. It was a good overhaul, and so life was, once again, good for surfer Mylan.

SELECTING AND BEING THE MARK

On your Mark, get set...

With only about a dozen *Overhaulin'* episodes aired during a single season, and with thousands of applications received during the year, selecting the Mark and his or her car can be difficult. After the initial screening, the prospective applicants are passed along to the show's producer, Bud Brutsman, supervising producer, Veronica Torres, and to the show's star, Chip Foose, for final approval.

The show's triumvirate then "read the applications for their car style and story value," says Veronica. "Once the Accomplice is interviewed and things look good, the Mark is selected. Bud and Chip look for car style, I go for the 'people' side of it. Then the network reads the proposed stories and approves them."

The heists and subsequent pranks played on the Marks are just as important to the show's success. "I love pranking people," says Bud, "but it's important that we do it in a dignified way so that nobody is embarrassed or made to feel bad."

Bud and his staff and the show's cohost, Chris Jacobs, conceive most of the pranks played on the Marks. "Chris helps concoct ideas," adds Bud, "and we rely on what the Insiders and Accomplices feel will push the Mark's button, too."

"We develop an intense relationship with the Insiders and Accomplices," adds Veronica. "We are in contact every day, via phone, text mail, e-mail, or visits to the shop. The Mark must be monitored and tracked for the entire week."

And when it all comes together—the pranks have been played and run their course, the A-Team has put the finishing touches on the car, and the time has come for the reveal—practically everybody on the *Overhaulin'* set and production crew is at an emotional high. "You can see it on the Marks' faces, too," explains Chip. "They're emotionally drained, and then when they see their car for the first time, the expression on their faces is, well, often priceless."

Yet with each episode concluded, the job only gets tougher for the production staff. Simply, the show's popularity has made Chip Foose and cohosts Chris Jacobs and Adrienne Janic (A. J.) familiar to people across the country, so stand-ins are often used to complete the pranks that once could be carried out by these members of the team.

"The pranks are getting tougher to do," concludes Bud, "because viewers are familiar with Chris and A. J.'s faces. They're also in tune to the ways of the *Overhaulin'* pranks." Which makes you wonder, will the *Overhaulin'* website one day have a link for submitting prank ideas?

One would get you two during the Double Haulin' episode in which the A-Team overhauled a car and truck belonging to two sisters. The Marks were Lindsay Cates and her 1968 Chevelle, and Chelsea Cates and her 1998 Mazda B3000 pickup.

Cassie Wyrick shows off the sketch for her 1991 Ford Explorer. Not only do the Marks get their cars overhauled, they also are presented with an authentic Chip Foose original—an artist rendering of the car as it was planned by Chip and the A-Team.

'68 CAMARO
Ian Ziering

A Cast of Thousands: Mark, Insider, Accomplice, and the A-Team

This particular episode was packed with Hollywood and automotive celebrities. While the mark, Ian Ziering, headed the marquee this time, he was joined by a costar from *Beverly Hills 90210*, whose role on *Overhaulin'* was that of an insider. Terry Cole, editor for *Super Chevy Magazine*, and Chip Foose represented the automotive contingent of celebrities, with Terry serving as the primary insider. Rounding out the cast of characters were shop owners Sal Perez and Jim Sleeper, who were accomplices to the prank as well as major players in the Camaro's overhaul. And they all helped make *902-Merlot* a vintage episode, one to remember.

I t's been said that it takes a thief to catch a thief, but in the case of overhaulin' this particular 1968 Camaro convertible, it took an actor to catch an actor. Actually, let's rephrase that: It took an actor and a car guy acting like an actor to catch an actor.

The actor, who also happened to be the *Overhaulin'* mark for Episode 105, was Ian Ziering. People familiar with the 1990s television smash hit *Beverly Hills 90210* recognize Ian as the actor who played the character Steve. One of Episode 105's insiders was Ian's *90210* costar, and he was joined by car-guy-cum-actor Terry Cole. Cole's daytime job? He's editor of *Super Chevy Magazine*, and through a common interest for Chevrolets, Cole had befriended Ian a few years before. But for seven special days Cole was going to turn on his Hollywood friend to conspire with Chip Foose's A-Team to overhaul Ian's basket-case 1968 Camaro convertible, which had been languishing in various auto shops for the past six years. The project had stalled for one reason or another until it

Left: While the car's deconstruction took place in Stitz Suspension's shop, Chip Foose took time to sketch, or "script," the concept onto paper for the final act.

Right: There it is, part of Ian Ziering's pride and joy before the overhaul. The remainder of the 1968 Camaro was in car shops scattered throughout Southern California. Hard to believe that in seven days this will be a finished car, ready for cruising. The biggest hurdle that confronted the A-Team was making the chassis right.

ended up in Jim Sleeper's shop, Sleeper Suspension Development. That's when the A-Team got the call, and with Priestley and Cole's help, they tricked Ian into believing that Sleeper's shop had been closed due to tax liens owed to the government. In an effort to garnish all that was owed the public, the "government" decided to attach all assets in the shop. That included Ian's car, or what there was of it to take.

That's when Cole got the curtain call from *Overhaulin'* producer Bud Brutsman to perform an insider role. Cole read his lines perfectly, too, explaining over the phone to Ian that they both had a vested interest in Sleeper's tax problem; both men had cars in the locked-up shop. Cole had convinced Ian, and about his own premier performance for the small screen, the magazine editor said: "Now I'm in his arena. Now I'm an actor."

A couple days later another call from Cole to Ian suggested that a tax attorney for the government could meet them at Sleeper's to discuss the situation. Played by *Overhaulin'*'s own resident actor, Chris Jacobs, the meeting

Summit supplied the crate motor, a fuel-injected small-block Chevrolet 350. The A-Team supplied the muscle and the know-how to install the engine and get it running.

Fabricating the custom center console proved to be a bigger project than expected. Work on the interior continued while the suspension crew readied the chassis.

accomplished little, other than Chris asking if Ian could help arrange an audition for his nephew who was an aspiring actor looking for a break. This, of course, pressed Ian's patience to the limits—just what the A-Team wanted.

But there was no playacting when Chip's cast of characters took to center stage to resurrect Ian's Camaro. The car was in pieces, its parts scattered in several shops throughout Southern California, among them Sleeper's suspension specialty shop, and Sal Perez's American Muscle Cars, where most of the overhaul actually took place. And what an overhaul it was going to be, because

Mike Lavallee is hot with the airbrush gun!
The realistic hot-lick flames were meticulously
applied, each one different than the next.
Graphics can make or break a project.

You can appreciate the time and talent that
went into the flames and graphics when you
look closely at this section of the hood. The devil
certainly is in the details.

the rolling chassis that had been con-
structed by a previous shop was
delivered to the A-Team looking
more like a dish of spaghetti than a
car frame. Worse yet, the half-cooked
frame was about as firm as over-
cooked pasta. With time working
against them, the decision was made

to try and salvage what they could of
the spaghetti frame, and deliver a car
that could handle corners like a rat
wearing new sneakers.

"All I'm trying to do (at this
point)," sighed Chip, "is get that car
put together again." Translation:
The A-Team had a rather daunting

task ahead of them, and perhaps seven days wasn't enough time to fulfill this script.

With the clock ticking, and Ian fuming, the A-Team got to work. By Day 2 they had the four-bar rear suspension figured out and tack welded. Precious time was also spent figuring out how to turn the spaghetti structure into a road-hugging automobile frame. Slowly—ever so slowly—the chassis came together, and with Sleeper working with Aaron Ohama, Jerod Meador, Rowland Gutierrez, Jerry Furgeson, and Andrew Shearer from Stitz Suspension, the mass of parts began to resemble a '68 Camaro convertible that would be like no other on Southern California's famous freeways.

While the suspension crew tackled that problem, not to mention shoehorning the small-block Chevy engine supplied by Summit into the engine bay, team members Rick Anderson and Krash faced the unenviable task of untangling the car's old wiring to accept a 3,500-watt sound system. Hmm, more spaghetti? Aaron succinctly summed up the situation when he volunteered while holding what appeared to be a ball of wires: "It looks like a big colorful mess." Yet

As the clock ticked closer to reveal time, everybody chipped in to give the Camaro its finishing touches. Sid and Kathy White chipped in to help complete the final details in minutes rather than hours.

Sitting down on the job? Nope, that's Hollywood actor and the Camaro's rightful owner, Ian Ziering, trying on the custom bucket seats for size and fit.

he and Krash somehow transformed the colorful mess into a mobile sound system powerful enough to blow Ian's socks off.

Meanwhile, backstage, Ian was in a quandary, unsure if he'd ever see his Camaro on the road, much less safe and sound back home in his garage. "This car's not meant to be," he lamented, convinced that the six-year project had become a lifetime albatross around his neck.

Day 7: Enter former *90210* costar, stage left. Actually he'll enter via cell phone because when Ian,

accompanied by Sleeper and Cole, show up one evening at a disclosed location to gather what remains of the '68 Camaro, the insider calls the mark to set up the reveal. After bantering back and forth, our insider finally lets the cat out of the bag, and the shop door is raised, revealing a Camaro convertible that didn't resemble, in the slightest, what viewers saw at the beginning of the program.

Among the Camaro's most striking features were the hot-lick flames that Chip laid out with painter Mike

Lavallee. The pyrotechnic graphics were stunning, leaving no doubt that this was one hot ride. Ian graciously accepted defeat, and the keys to his car, still not sure that this was, indeed, the same heap of parts that took up floor space in several SoCal speed shops only a few days before.

As an epilogue, Ian now cruises the California beaches in the car of his dreams, Cole retained his day job to produce some of the best Chevrolet-related magazines on the newsstands today, Chip and the A-Team moved on to further conquests, and Chris' "cousin" never did get that audition.

The Camaro is finished and ready for inspection. The A-Team's big concern throughout the project was whether the car would be ready for its reveal at the appointed time.

'56 CHEVROLET BEL AIR
Dale Eslinger

Dale Eslinger

As head of the WyoTech Foundation, Dale Eslinger had been entrusted with the school's recently donated 1956 Chevrolet while the auto shop was to be fumigated. That was the story that the WyoTech staff told him, anyway. In reality, they were setting Dale up for the heist. And for seven days, Chip Foose and the A-Team had Dale sweating bullets when the local police department—who participated in the sting—showed signs of making Dale one of their suspects. For *Overhaulin'* viewers, it was one hour of fun and drama, but for Dale it turned out to be one week of headache and heartburn.

E pisode 106 might go down as the *Overhaulin'* A-Team's finest hour. That was the one-hour episode in which the team—their ranks bolstered with students and faculty members from WyoTech, one of the leading trade-technical institutes in the country—transformed an all-original 1956 Chevrolet Bel Air four-door sedan into a stunning show-quality two-door open-top speedster. And they did it within the seven-day

In its as-is condition, the 50-year-old Bel Air's interior was in decent shape. As one A-Team member pointed out, the dashboard was certainly useable.

time frame that's unique to *Overhaulin'*. It was a specialty-car-build that merits milestone status.

The episode began innocently enough when Chip Foose and *Overhaulin'* co-host Courtney Hansen "stole" the Chevy in broad daylight from the mark's

WyoTech Students and Staff

This was a slightly different episode because the overhauled car really didn't belong to the mark. The 1956 Chevrolet Bel Air had been donated to WyoTech so the students could use it for a project car. And the students—and some of WyoTech's staff and alumni—got to do just that when the *Overhaulin'* crew came to town. They converted the four-door sedan into a two-door speedster, and the result was one of the most unique cars ever built on *Overhaulin'*.

driveway. The mark was Dale Eslinger, head of the WyoTech Foundation, and the man who happened to be entrusted with the car's well-being while—to Dale's knowledge—the school's auto shop was to be fumigated. The Chevy was school property, a donation from a private individual who intended the old Bel Air to be a project car for the auto shop students. WyoTech's faculty had asked Dale if he wouldn't mind babysitting the car for a few days until the fumigation was completed. Enter Chip and Courtney, who staged the car's theft, sprinkling broken glass chips on the driveway as "evidence" of their caper. In reality, they simply used the ignition key to start the Chevy and drive it away.

Chip said to Courtney, who sat in the driver's seat, "Here's your key."

By the third day, the transformation into a two-door speedster was apparent. Despite the progress, the A-Team had a long way to go before its reveal on Day 7.

With the rear bucket seats formed and ready for upholstery, Chip asked Jerry to put them in place for a final fit before the fabricators could recess the rear deck panel.

Courtney replied coyly, "You're so stealth." And then they quietly drove off, taking the four-door Bel Air directly to WyoTech for its seven-day overhaul. Within two hours, the doors were removed, the interior was gutted, the engine was pulled, and the top was completely chopped. Six days and 22 hours remained to complete the conversion.

With such an ambitious goal, Chip recruited one of the top metal fabricators in the country, Troy Trepanier, for assistance. Troy was joined by his ace fabricator Levi Green, and for good measure Chip brought along his right-hand man in the shop, Bryan Fuller. Coincidentally, Levi and Bryan were both WyoTech graduates.

The two WyoTech alumni were greeted by some familiar faces in the shop. Several faculty members volunteered to help, including, Mike (paint), Wayne (chassis), Darrel (engine), Jerry (interior), and Gary (dyno). They were complemented by a small squadron of future WyoTech grads, taking the A-Team to 33 members. Given

With the sheet-metal work finished, the body was given its first coat of primer at WyoTech's paint shop. The next challenge facing the A-Team was the two-tone paint job.

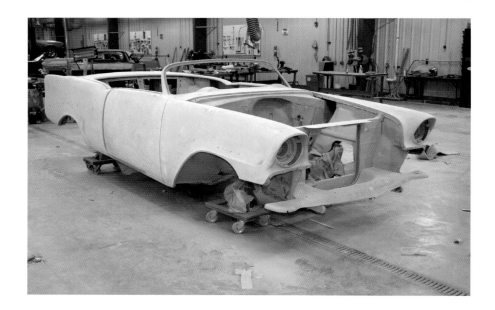

Chip is a master with the airbrush. On the Bel Air, he illustrated how to airbrush graphics, making them look like chromed badges.

the extent of this overhaul, all hands would be needed if they were to beat the clock for the reveal.

Of course, no overhaul is complete unless the mark is made to sweat for seven days, so the prank that put Dale in the hot seat involved the Laramie Police Department. With their help, and the assistance of police officer, Jeff Bury, a new investigator joined the force—"Officer Jacobs," played by co-host Chris Jacobs. It was his job to guide the investigation so the long finger of the law would point to Dale as a possible suspect. And as Dale squirmed like a worm on a hook, the A-Team got to work, hustling day and night to make the deadline.

The coolest cucumber in the bunch was Chip, who, when mapping out the overhaul during the strategy meeting with his 32 coconspirators, said, "We're not worried about the top because we're going to get rid of it." He said this as if he were an auto mechanic talking about a 10-minute

Ace fabricator Troy Trepanier settles in behind the rear cross-member and differential housing to inspect how things are progressing with the chassis.

oil change. There was also the matter of fabricating two new doors to fill the gap the A-Team created by sealing up both rear doors, laying out a whole new interior with four bucket seats and a full-length center console, reshaping the front fascia and grille work, rebuilding the entire chassis, and shoehorning a big-block V-8

Believe it or not, these graphics were painted by hand. Using 3-D effects, Chip created what look like factory-installed name badges, in this case "Speed Air" emblems.

engine under the hood. That didn't take into account fitting a modified rear windshield from a 1949 Mercury to serve as the speedster's new windshield, or painting the car a stunning two-tone scheme with air-brushed 3-D graphics on the side panels. Then there was the issue of keeping Dale preoccupied so he couldn't find time to drop by the school's auto shop and spoil the surprise.

One way to keep Dale out of the shop was to keep him busy in the office. With the help of Denise, the WyoTech Foundation's office manager, Officer Jacobs kept Dale guessing, and he never once suspected that the school's

Even though the dashboard was given its own overhaul, the A-Team retained its classic 1950s-era charm. This two-door speedster seats four passengers in four bucket seats.

When your car is a speedster, with emphasis on "speed," it had better have some muscle under the hood. The Speed Air speedster relies on a Chevrolet big-block for punch.

staff and student body were part of the prank. Instead, he was led to believe the car had been stolen, stripped, and sold by a band of car thieves.

Finally, it was time for the reveal. Officer Jacobs called Dale to report that the car had been recovered and returned to the school. Jacobs asked Dale to meet with him so they could confirm that the pile of parts on the trailer was, indeed, the remains of the car that had been stolen from his driveway seven days earlier.

Dale was speechless as he examined the parts stacked on the trailer. His nightmare had come true, but little did he know that Officer Jacobs was about to show Dale the dream ride that the WyoTech students and faculty members had built. The parts on the trailer were, in fact, all the junk that the A-Team had discarded.

When Dale viewed the overhauled Chevy for the first time, he was speechless. Finally, he muttered, "You did all this in seven days? Amazing." Then came the real treat— one by one the A-Team members walked into the room to pay their respects to the man who had done so much to help keep WyoTech at the forefront of the trade school industry. Class dismissed.

SHOW CO-HOSTS

Think of Them as the Acting Team

Although the A-Team receives their share of accolades for the cars they build, just as important to the show's success are the co-hosts. They are the people called upon to keep the Marks off balance so they remain unaware of the overhaul in progress. Their job includes posing as various characters who interact with the Marks, either by telephone or in person, confusing them enough so they can't track down their cars.

The show's first two seasons were co-hosted by Chris Jacobs and Courtney Hansen. Both could be labeled as qualified gearheads, too. Chris describes himself as being "obsessed with hot rods," while Courtney's father was a multi-champion road racer who taught his daughter all he could about cars. Both are from the Midwest, Chris hailing from Chicago, Courtney from Minnesota.

Although Chris graduated from law school and passed the California bar in 1995, his true passion is acting. He has credits on various television programs including *The X-Files*, *CSI*, *Touched by an Angel*, and *Two and a Half Men*. Quite often he dons a disguise that allows him to confront the Marks in person, making for some interesting, and often humorous, scenes.

Likewise, Courtney's television career began before she appeared on *Overhaulin'*. After receiving a bachelor of arts degree in marketing from Florida State University, she served as a spokesperson in a series of television commercials for Dodge, and later hosted a TV comedy show about golf. But it was Courtney's robust smile and unbridled enthusiasm on *Overhaulin'* that ultimately put her in the limelight within the automotive community. She left the show after two seasons to pursue other endeavors, vacating her spot to Adrienne Janic, who goes by the nickname A. J.

A. J.'s on-camera experience runs just as deep as Chris and Courtney's before their *Overhaulin'* days. She's appeared in numerous commercials, and her work as a photo model took her to Europe, Asia, Africa, and all across America. She hosted several shows on E! Entertainment, and landed the role as host of a pilot called *The Music Café* prior to joining Chris Jacobs as cohost on *Overhaulin'* at the end of 2005.

While the success of *Overhaulin'* clearly hinges on how successful the A-Team performs in the shop, there's no doubt that the show's cohosts play instrumental roles in the program's ratings with the television audience. They are, in truth, the voices of the show.

Chris Jacobs, a man of a thousand faces, seen here under disguise

Courtney Hansen is no stranger to the automotive world—her father was a multi-champion amateur road racer.

Adrienne Janic, (middle) otherwise known as A. J., joined the show for its third season.

'64 CORVETTE
Connie "C. J." Eastman

Connie "C. J." Eastman

Connie doesn't describe herself as an avowed gearhead, but she knows a landmark car when she sees—and owns—one. And her 1964 Corvette fastback coupe is a classic, one she's owned since high school. At about the time she and her husband, Pete, began raising a family, the 'Vette fell into disrepair and needed some attention. Connie's also a stickler for detail, and it was her attention to the little things that prompted her to check out the alleged police investigating team that showed up at her garage to sort through the evidence of the heist. Luckily, she didn't find out the truth, and for the remainder of the week she was in the dark as to her 'Vette's whereabouts.

If you were to go out to your garage right now, chances are you'd have to wade through clutter that includes more than a few throwaway items that, for various reasons, have evaded the Dumpster. And if you're like some car enthusiasts, you might even have an old car sitting under wraps—usually beneath a tarp, old blanket, or car cover—that's waiting the green light to project-car status. But until that time, the car and clutter collect dust while you go about your daily tasks.

Connie "C. J." Eastman and her husband, Pete, had such a garage. Parked among the dirt bikes, empty picture frames, and broken lawnmowers sat Connie's 1964 Corvette, a car that was handed down to her by her father. Connie's dad was the 'Vette's second owner, and he gave it to her as a high school graduation present in 1972. It sat forlornly in the garage, awaiting

Father-and-son day at the shop: Sam Foose (right) oversees his son Chip begin modifications to the Moon Equip quick-fill gas cap lid for Connie's Corvette. By week's end, Chip couldn't say enough good things about his dad.

Pete Eastman

Connie's husband was all for Chip Foose's A-Team restoring her 1964 Corvette. He was also the ringleader for the heist and had to keep Connie busy on a wild-goose chase while the A-Team finished their weekly chores. What he didn't know, however, was that Chip Foose had his eye on Pete's own hobby car, a Volkswagen Thing that still sported its original 1970s-era paint and upholstery. Chip and company had hauled it away with the rest of the garage clutter, but while Pete thought his car was sitting out of the way in Steve LuVisi's parking lot, truth was that Foose had ordered new paint and upholstery for it for a "double overhaul." Mission accomplished, and the Eastmans rode into the sunset with two overhauled vehicles.

Steve LuVisi (right) has been restoring and repairing Corvettes for years. This week-long project was to be LuVisi's 100th frame-off restoration. It also turned out to be the quickest such project he's ever undertaken.

resurrection, for about 10 years before Chip Foose and the A-Team hijacked it for overhaul. Perhaps that should be rephrased to Chip Foose and his A-*Plus* Team, because Chip's father, Sam, came out of retirement to help out on this episode. And at 70 years young, the senior Foose, who's a legend among old-school hot rodders, had plenty of experience and shop savvy to share with the A-Team.

The insider for this episode was Connie's husband, Pete, who oversaw the heist that, it turned out, included a

A frame-off restoration means just that—removing the body from the frame. The crew at Lanzini Body Works repaired the 41-year-old fiberglass body. Working with fiberglass is tricky because the resin needs to dry thoroughly.

complete clean out of the garage. The plan was to make it look like grand theft auto, and just so there was no mistaking the intentions of the thieves, the A-Team hauled *everything* from the garage in a moving van that was labeled, fittingly, Haulin' Moving Company. They left only a few dust balls on a bare concrete floor. The thieves included show hosts Chris Jacobs and Courtney Hansen, fabricator Bryan Fuller, Sam and Chip, upholstery artists Mitch Lanzini and Carl Richmond, Corvette specialist Steve LuVisi, and special guest Camee Edelbrock from Edelbrock Performance. Explained Chris to the camera for Connie's benefit: "Not only are you going to get your car overhauled, you're getting your garage cleaned out."

The clean out was the easy part. Back at LuVisi's shop, Automotive Expertise Unlimited, the A-Team decided to give the old 'Vette a complete frame-off restoration—in

Sam Foose (left) is among hot rodding's most respected car builders. He came out of retirement to help with this project. Camee Edelbrock (right) is a third-generation gearhead—her grandfather, Vic Sr., formed the company, Edelbrock Performance, in 1941.

Unwanted Garage Sale

The plan was simple—the A Team would pose as movers who were sent in to literally clean out Connie Eastman's garage of its contents, which included her 1964 Corvette. When the "theft" was reported, Chris Jacobs and his team of investigators reported right away, hoping to convince Connie that her Corvette had been stolen by an experienced ring of car thieves. The hook almost didn't set, prompting Connie to call the Fullerton Police Department to verify Chris's existence on the force.

As LuVisi pointed out, one of the most critical points in a Corvette frame-off restoration is putting the delicate fiberglass body back onto the frame. The body is slowly lowered into position to make sure it's square at all points.

seven days. Corvette enthusiasts know that this is no easy task; fitting the fiberglass body back onto the steel frame has to be a delicate procedure to ensure that the "plastic" body doesn't crack or break in the process. Fortunately, Luvisi is no stranger to frame-offs, and as it turned out, this was to be a milestone restoration for him: Connie's Corvette would be LuVisi's 100th such body-off project.

Under LuVisi's direction, A-Team members gently plucked the fiberglass shell from its frame, then ordered a wealth of parts from Long Island Corvette Supply and Mid-America Corvette for Saturday morning delivery. While Chip made it known that he intended to duplicate a styling trick his dad taught him years ago for the fastback Corvette's classic gas cap, LuVisi tore apart the car's tired small-block V-8 engine for

Ask any gearhead and he'll tell you that the heartbeat of any car is the engine. And so, when it came to pumping new life into Connie's Corvette, Edelbrock Performance sent over a new crate engine to replace the original small-block V-8.

inspection. What they found inside wasn't promising. There were bits of metal at the bottom of the oil pan, prompting the A-Team to make an executive decision—rebuild the aging V-8, or transplant a new crate motor into the engine bay.

Camee Edelbrock spoke up, suggesting that Chip call her dad, Vic Jr., back at Edelbrock HQ for help. Chip whipped out his trusty cell phone, dialed Vic's number, greeting him with a cheery "Uncle Vic," then politely asked for a new engine. Brief pause while Vic replies, then Chip echoes his response, "*Anything* we want? That's great. You're the best!" Next day an Edelbrock crate motor arrived for installation. So simple.

Indeed, this episode revealed some deep-rooted bonds between gearhead fathers and their motorhead children. Turns out that Chip was seven years old when he began working on cars with his dad, and as a member of the famed Edelbrock family, Camee has maintained a close relationship with her dad since she grasped her first steering wheel. Most of all, though, the star of this episode—the '64 Corvette— has served as Connie's connection to her father, Jewel Eastin, since he passed away a few years ago.

While LuVisi oversaw the work on the chassis, Lanzini's crew tackled restoring the fiberglass body, SW Performance Transmissions readied a new shift box for the drivetrain,

Various replacement parts were culled from Long Island Corvette Supply and Mid-America. Fiber Technology reupholstered the car's interior, often taking their measurements while working around the rest of the A-Team.

Fiber Technology measured and cut fabric for the upholstery, and Chip went to the drawing board to design a paint scheme for the BASF paint they would mix. The fiberglass body proved especially troublesome to restore, prompting Jacobs to say, "The A-Team went from twenty-four-hour days to twenty-five-hour days." And if that wasn't enough, Chip decided to roll Pete's semi-restored Volkswagen Thing, a mid-1970s runabout from Germany, down the road to Anaheim Hills Auto Body for its own little overhaul of new paint and upholstery. The 25-hour days just got longer.

Although the body doesn't sport any major modifications, it has subtle features to make it look better. Bryan Fuller gave the bumpers a tighter fit, in turn emphasizing the Sting Ray's classic lines.

The 1964 Corvette fastback is considered a classic by car aficionados the world over. For this project, Chip Foose decided to give the flip-up gas cap beneath the rear window a treatment that his dad, Sam, perfected years ago.

But extra work didn't deter the A-Plus Team, and before the week was over, the restored body was ceremoniously lowered onto the refurbished frame that now housed a brand-new Edelbrock small-block Chevrolet engine. But there was one problem: the engine refused to fire to life when given the order. Enter Steve Breninger from Foose's shop to help LuVisi locate the spark that was necessary to breathe life into the engine. With moments to spare before the reveal, they succeeded, and the burble through the Bassani exhausts was music to everybody's ears. After a 15-minute idle to help break in the engine's moving parts, LuVisi switched off the ignition to wait for Connie and Pete for the reveal.

The reveal itself was a reunion, of sorts, for Connie, her car, and her late father. It also proved that, if you wait long enough, even a cluttered garage will eventually just go away.

'67 CHEVY II NOVA
Katy Eyer

Scott, Katy
and
Pam Eyer

The family that pranks together cranks together. Katy (center) takes a breather after the reveal with her brother Scott and mother Pam. Before the heist, Katy's intentions were to keep the Nova for many years. After the overhaul you can bet she'll keep that promise to herself.

There comes a time when enough is enough. And for the A-Team and Katy Eyer, seven days proved time enough before patience and tempers showed signs of boiling over.

The episode began innocently enough, with a rather uneventful heist of Katy's 1967 Chevrolet Chevy II Nova. With inside help from Katy's brother, Scott, the A-Team disabled the car so she couldn't drive it to work one day. The setup was to render the Nova inoperable during "sweep day," when the city street sweepers clear the curbside gutters of debris. No cars could be parked on the street at that time. Insider Scott had covertly removed the ignition coil wire from Katy's car so the Nova's tired six-cylinder engine wouldn't start. Left with no choice but to leave the car in front of her apartment where she normally parks it overnight, Katy posted a note on her windshield kindly asking the parking patrol not to ticket her. "Please don't ticket me. My car won't start," read the note. Through grace and luck, Katy was only issued a warning, but her luck ended

Members of the Overhaulin' A-Team line up in Dagel's Rod 'n' Truck to begin the overhaul of Katy Eyer's 1967 Nova. This overhaul turned out to be tougher than expected.

Not a bad looking old Nova. Little did crew members suspect the horror that lurked beneath the bronze paint.

there. Moments later, Scott and *Overhaulin'* co-host Courtney Hansen discreetly replaced the coil wire, and then drove the car to Dagel's Rod 'n' Truck where the bronze-colored Nova would be overhauled by Chip Foose and the A-Team.

As always, Chip's A-Team lineup for this episode included some very experienced personnel. Wyoming Tech Institute—among the nation's leading automotive technical schools—sent instructor Brock Oreck and A-student Jessi Combs to help out, and Stitz Street Rods loaned experienced hands Roland Gutierrez and Aaron Ohama. To help with parts acquisition as much as the

After a complete teardown, the Overhaulin' crew discovered more rust and body filler than they reckoned. Century Collision Center in Orange, California, applied the paint and graphics.

Chip Foose exhibits tireless energy. Although he helps with the physical work, he also takes time out to sketch the redesign for the car, finishing in a matter of minutes.

overhaul itself, Ashley Sangster, whose daytime job is owner of Classic Industries, joined in. Classic Industries has a catalog chock full of replacement parts for Novas, so his presence was invaluable. Naturally, Gary Dagel—owner of Dagel's Rod 'n' Truck—and Chip Foose were there to fill out the A-Team's management.

The game plan also included Jan Van Kooten's needle-and-thread crew at Stitch by Stitch for upholstery, and Century Collision Center would follow through on the paint after Chip decided on the color and graphics.

As deconstruction began, hopes ran high for a quick and easy overhaul. Viewed from 10 feet away

Believe it or not, in addition to her other Overhaulin' duties, co-host Courtney Hansen can wield a spray gun. She painted the small-block engine that Guaranty Chevrolet brought. Here Chip Foose gives the engine a few final touches.

Katy's 1967 Nova was given a set of specially built one-off wheels designed exclusively for the car by Chip Foose.

the Nova appeared fairly straight and rust-free. It would be a simple matter of stripping the body to prep its sheet metal, masking it for graphics, then applying the finish coats. Slam dunk and done. Stitch by Stitch could easily address the interior, and Guaranty Chevrolet was scheduled to deliver a brand-new 350 engine to replace the sad six that sat in the engine bay.

But the groundswell of enthusiasm flattened when the weathered top coat was stripped, revealing splotches of rust in hard-to-reach places, and thick layers of body filler—some up to a half-inch thick—beneath the belt line. Chip expressed concern that maybe this overhaul was going to take more effort and time than expected.

None of that really concerned Chris Jacobs. His job was to keep Katy guessing. She was told that the Nova had been impounded by the city because it was blocking the lane for the street sweeper. Chris, posing as the tow yard

Jan Van Kooten's crew at Stitch by Stitch reupholstered the Nova's interior. Chip Foose wanted to give the car a retro theme, using fabric popular 40 or 50 years ago.

owner, called Katy to apologize for the injustice—it was a case of mistaken identity for another car that had several unpaid parking violations. Chris apologized to Katy for the city's miscue, stating that the car would be returned after the necessary paperwork was completed. In the meantime, he suggested, perhaps he and she could "get together for a cup of coffee or something." Taken aback, Katy opted to pass on this idea, suggesting to him that his behavior was unprofessional. After hanging up the phone Chris turned to the *Overhaulin'* camera and said, "Do I have a way with the ladies, or what?"

The cat-and-mouse games—Katy chasing her car, and Chris chasing Katy—grew more intense as the episode developed. The next day when Chris delivered what appeared to be Katy's car covered and on a tow truck, she recognized that it was not her car. More tension and drama, and Katy was, by now, losing patience.

The paint theme that Chip Foose chose focused on stemmed cherries like those tattooed on Katy's left arm. The graphics shown here on the car's beltline matched perfectly.

Emotionally drained, and somewhat stunned at the reveal, a happy Katy Eyer gets to sit in her Nova for the first time in a week. The heist and sting went off without a hitch.

Chris checked the paperwork again, and "realized" that Katy's car had mistakenly been sent to San Diego. In the course of the visit, he again suggested that they might get together at a later time when this mess was cleared up. Not only couldn't Katy believe that her car was in transit to San Diego, but she found it unbelievable that Chris would even consider making a date with her.

Meanwhile, back at Dagel's the overhaul was going slower than expected. Having gained more insight into Katy's personality, Chip settled on a color scheme and graphic theme, stating, "The vision I have is 1930s Hollywood." The styling theme also tied to the tattoo—two stemmed cherries—that Katy has on her left arm. As the final topping to the car, Chip had Oreck form a cherry-shaped fastener nut for the engine's air cleaner.

With reveal day fast approaching, Chip told Scott that it was time to bring his sister down to the shop. "Bring her down emotionally," said Chip, "and bring her down physically to Orange County [for the reveal]."

That didn't stop Chris "the Cad" from making one more pass, this time in the parking lot where the reveal would take place. Courtney helped with the sting this time, posing as the truck driver delivering the car—and also as a woman who Chris had hit on in the past. Courtney and Katy immediately bonded, sharing horror stories about Chris' advances while the hidden *Overhaulin'* camera rolled, catching it all on tape.

It was time for one last prank, and again Katy was shown a bronze Nova that wasn't hers. On the brink of tears, Chris and Courtney confessed what was going on. It was perhaps one of the best stings yet by the *Overhaulin'* crew. Katy was taken completely off guard. Mission accomplished, and there would be time enough for her to enjoy the ride for years to come.

'68 OLDSMOBILE 4-4-2
Chris Franchimone

Chris Franchimone

Chris is described as a man whose family comes first. He's also a diehard gearhead who's owned his hobby car for 24 years. But, family comes first, so the Oldsmobile 4-4-2 has played second fiddle to family functions and expenses. But now that the Olds has been overhauled, you can bet that the car is a vested member of the Franchimone family.

Several years before General Motors' Oldsmobile car division met its Waterloo, the beleaguered brand staged a marketing strategy with the slogan: "Not your father's Oldsmobile." The goal was to attract younger buyers, something Oldsmobile hadn't done since the muscle car–era when it offered the fabled 4-4-2 and the colorful Hurst/Olds packages. Unfortunately, the "not your father's Olds" ad campaign failed. By 2003, what was, at the time, the oldest automobile marque in America, had taken a one-way street to the big parking lot in the sky.

But none of that had any effect on Chris Franchimone, who owned a 1968 Oldsmobile 4-4-2. If Chris had his way, his personal slogan could be: "This is my grandmother's Oldsmobile." You see, Grandma Franchimone—the car's original owner—had given the keys to Chris

The Franchimone family and friends share a final timeout before Chris fires up the Olds 4-4-2 for its maiden trip home, where it will assume its allotted place within this car-loving clan.

Jennifer Franchimone, Scott McClintock, and Brian Newman

For many years, Jennifer admired her husband's devotion to this family heirloom. Now it's her turn to take care of Chris and his car. She did so with the help of Scott, their neighbor, and Chris' best friend, Brian. You can bet that Brian gets to sit shotgun when it's time for Chris and the Olds to attend a local cruise night!

when he reached driving age in 1980. Moreover, Oldsmobile offered only 4,282 of these cars in 1968, making this 4-4-2 a rare ride. Chris vowed to never let the classic car leave the Franchimone fold.

So when Chris' wife Jennifer marked the Olds for an overhaul by Chip Foose and company, she stipulated that the car could not lose its muscle car–era character. "No problem," said Chip, who recognized the car's historical link to an era many car enthusiasts consider the zenith of Motown's muscle madness. Chip would incorporate his own special styling tricks, but not tamper with the Oldsmobile's heritage. "When people see it [finished]," said Chip during the build, "they'll know it's the *Overhaulin'* Olds."

Like the overhaul, the heist would be a straightforward affair: Chris' friend and neighbor, and soon-to-be-insider, Scott McClintock had agreed to paint the car using another friend's shop for the final prep and paint. Chris entrusted the 4-4-2 to Scott, who was to drive the aging muscle car to the paint shop. It never got there.

Well, at least to that paint shop. The usual *Overhaulin'* suspects, co-hosts Chris Jacobs and Courtney Hansen, intervened and drove the car to MagnaFlow's shop in Rancho Santa Margarita, California, for its one-week overhaul. Knowing that the car was in for a complete facelift, Chris and Courtney used the occasion for a joy ride. "We burned some rubber on our way to MagnaFlow," bragged Chris into the camera, referring to the handful of burn-outs he performed on the way. Added Courtney, for the mark's sake, "We're having so much fun stealing your car!" The "fun" lasted until the upper radiator hose blew, prompting the engine to overheat. "Oops," said our coconspirators, who were stranded alongside the road until things cooled down, leaving the A-Team to wait patiently at MagnaFlow for the car to show up.

Lying in wait were some experienced car guys itching to start the overhaul. The A-Team consisted of: MagnaFlow's Adam Diaz, Richard Waitas, Marko Milosevich, and Darron Shubin, who were joined by Jeff "Grumpy" Ferina (Original Parts Group), Craig Chaffers

Left: Chip uses the white board each episode to map out his strategy for the A-Team to follow. And before he's finished with his instructions, the white board gains color of its own.

Right: The A-Team initially thought this overhaul would be a slam-dunk. But after the paint was stripped, they found what fabricator Matt Harris described charitably as "rust and such."

The vinyl top has been ripped off, the A-Team lowered the chassis' undercarriage to the floor, and the interior was gutted long ago. Yep, looks like a typical Overhaulin' *car on Day 1.*

(C&C Designs), fabricator Matt Harris, and Charlie Tissen (K&N Air Filters). Chip Foose was lead, and the entire team called on Jacobs and Hansen for moral—and sometimes verbal—support. Jacobs would also serve as the primary force behind the prank they planned to play on Chris for the next seven days.

But first let's take a look at Chris' car after the A-Team completely gutted it on MagnaFlow's clean and spacious shop floor. First thing the gang found was more rust and corrosion than expected. Naturally the classic 4-4-2's signature 400-cubic-inch engine would remain, although it was given the once-over to make sure it fired on all cylinders.

Part of the prank required the A-Team to fake a few "theft" photos of the car for Chris' benefit. To do this, the A-Team had some more fun, stripping the car and spraying graffiti on the carcass. A few snapshots served as "evidence" of the recovered car that would later be shown to Chris. Chip went the full nine yards, too, creating a fake crack in the windshield by running lines of thin tape in jagged spurts.

Chris' long-time friend Brian Newman was called upon to help as well. His role was to engage Chris in a few telephone calls to discuss the disappearance of the car. Brian lent a sympathetic ear while Chris lamented the fate of his Olds. "He is convinced, hook, line, and sinker," Brian said later.

Sure, it's all smiles for the camera now, but behind Foose's façade is a serious A-Team player. The dust on his shirt is evidence that Chip gets down and dirty just like the rest of the crew.

Chip Foose has an eye for all kinds of cars, including classic muscle cars. And so, to play on the 4-4-2's heritage, he retained the classic front-quarter-panel stripes on Chris' car.

Scott also talked with Chris about the car's disappearance. Chris volunteered that he didn't "care if it's painted or not. I don't care if it's in pieces. I just want it back." To which Chris Jacobs replied into the *Overhaulin'* camera: "He doesn't care if it's painted. He doesn't care if it's in pieces. Hey, we could hand it back to him right now. That's where it's at—in pieces."

Left: Muscle cars from the 1960s are known for their go power, but most of them had drum brakes, which means they didn't stop very well. Baer disc brakes on all four corners mean that Chris' 4-4-2 will actually stop as well as it goes.

Right: Intro Wheels supplied the semi-retro five-spoke wheels on B.F. Goodrich rubber. You can appreciate the size of those Baer brake rotors in this photo. You also get an idea of how low the car sits.

Of course, Jacobs failed to mention that some new, and rather cool, pieces were also finding their way onto the car as well. Collision Care Centers applied the paint and Chip Foose graphics, and Stitchcraft Interiors reupholstered the seats. Members from Hotchkis Suspension and Baer Brakes were busy with the undercarriage, and after they finished, MagnaFlow added the exhaust.

Time for the reveal, but before that, Jacobs got into costume to pose as the clerk at the tow yard where Chris' "recovered" car sat. Jacobs played the unsympathetic clerk perfectly, informing Chris that the body had been accidentally sent to the wrecking yard where it was to be crushed.

Chris himself felt crushed by this news, and Jacobs only added to his woes, suggesting that the car wasn't worth salvaging. Chris defended his car, but before he lost his cool, Jacobs called in his "supervisor," who, it turned out, was Courtney Hansen. Turns out, too, that Chris was a big fan of *Overhaulin'*, and immediately recognized her.

The prank was over, and it was one of the most heart-warming reveals in the show's history. A real car lover had been caught, as his best friend said, "hook, line, and sinker."

We also got to witness the quasi-restoration of a classic automobile. This 4-4-2 truly is Chris Franchimone's Oldsmobile.

There was no debate about retaining the classic 400-cubic-inch Olds engine, but the A-Team dressed it with new-millennium colors. That colorful air cleaner is a free-flow unit from K&N Air Filters.

'70 CHEVY MONTE CARLO
Rayce Denton

Rayce Denton

Sometimes a car enthusiast has to choose between restoring his ride and keeping the cupboards stocked for the family. There was never a choice for Rayce, who always put his family first and everything else second. Even so, the 1970 Monte Carlo that his father gave him remained in the family—it just didn't enjoy the same privileges as the other members. The A-Team changed that, and now, you might say, the Denton family is complete. The 1970 Monte Carlo got the full Monty, and now it's ready to assume its role for family outings.

W here there's smoke, there's fire. Or so we've been told. And for this episode, the smoke started billowing into the sky when the chosen *Overhaulin'* mark, Rayce Denton, was told that his 1970 Chevrolet Monte Carlo had been the object of a theft, and was later caught in the middle of a back-alley gunfight. At first, Rayce took the news rather stoically, but then Chris Jacobs, in the guise of a law officer named McKay, informed Rayce that he was a police suspect in the shootout. The smoke started getting thicker and thicker on the horizon, and for the remainder of the seven-day rebuild, smoke got in Rayce Denton's eyes.

The fire? That would be Rayce's 1970 Monte Carlo, a car that was handed down to him by his father, who had purchased it new back in the days of leaded gasoline and bias-ply tires. You see, the Monte got its nickname *Fire Car* from Rayce's son, Rayce Jr. The car's loud, rumbling exhaust made it sound, in Rayce Jr.'s mind, like a fire engine, hence the nickname *Fire Car*.

Believe it or not, Rayce was rather proud of the Monte's vinyl top! These roof covers were popular back in the 1960s and 1970s. The A-Team planned to bring this top into the new millennium.

But Rayce wanted to change that. One day he'd give his car the full Monty, so the Chevy would not only look cool, but its exhaust note would sound more like that of a refined, restored automobile. That day was a long way off—Rayce had a family to raise, and they came first.

Then Rayce's wife Linda contacted Chip Foose's gang at *Overhaulin'*, suggesting that the aging, but fully intact Monte Carlo would be a prime candidate for deconstruction and reconstruction. The A-Team rushed into action, but only after Chris and Courtney Hansen drove the car to Extreme Automotive Incorporated for its overhaul. During the drive to Extreme, Chris confided to the *Overhaulin'* camera, "This car is in one sad and sorry state. It's so bad, there's no time to lose. This thing's a hunk of junk." Rayce's ears must have been burning.

Junk or no, the A-Team was fired up and ready to get going on the car. In terms of personnel, Rayce—even

A little makeup can go a long way. In this case, the makeup enabled Chip Foose to play the role of a homeless person who was a witness to the "shootout" in the alley.

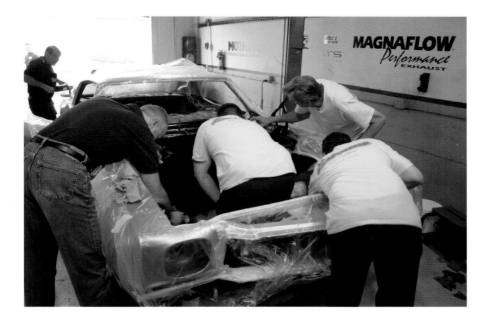

As with all overhauls, every nook and cranny in the car is inspected and treated. Before installing the ZZ4 engine, the engine bay was given the once-over.

though he didn't know it at the time—had some of the most experienced car hands on the job. Extreme offered Sean Roberts and his father, Tim "Poppy" Roberts, who were joined by Sal Gutierrez. Primo Customs, which was in charge of the body prep and paint, was represented by Ricky and Tommy Primeau. The A-Team was supplemented with builders Richard "Pappa" Primeau and Craig Chaffers, and Noone Interiors offered Jerry and J. J. Noone and Eric Nisbet to give the Monte an interior that Chip described as an "upscale facelift only." In short, he wanted to retain the integrity of the Monte Carlo's crew's quarters, yet give it the zing that all the *Overhaulin'* cars were known for.

The "hunk of junk" Monte Carlo was to receive more than just a facelift inside and out, though. It was also going to get new muscle in the form of an out-of-the-crate ZZ4 engine from Guaranty Chevrolet. But wait, there's more—Vortech was sending over a bolt-on supercharger system that would give the fabled ZZ4 another 120 or so horsepower. If this power package didn't light Rayce's fire, nothing would.

Extreme Automotive's trio—Sal Guitierrez, Tim "Poppy" Roberts, and Sean Roberts— tackled the Monte Carlo's undercarriage. Art Carr supplied the 200 R4 transmission.

Some of the body panel's rust and cor- rosion had to be treated from both sides. When the body was ready for paint and graphics, it was wheeled over to Primo Customs.

But before there was to be ignition, the A-Team had to blast off all the old and weathered parts from the Monte Carlo's tired body and chassis. That, it turned out, proved to be tougher than the A-Team first expected. The restoration process took so long that it wasn't until 2 p.m. of Day 6 that the car finally rolled into Primo Customs' paint booth for its first coat of primer. By 5 a.m. the following morning, though, Chip and company had the ghost-flame graphics applied and drying! As Courtney said in the course of the build, the A-Team was "taking the car from late to great."

Indeed, it was looking great, and as the pieces of the puzzle came together, the Monte Carlo was beginning to look more like Monte Fuego—Mount Fire. When Linda returned to the shop to inspect the

Although it's a lot of work to rebuild a car in seven days, there's a sense of accomplishment involved, too. It also helps when the car is spotless, inside and out!

The GM performance motor, from Guaranty Chevrolet—a potent ZZ4 Chevrolet 350—is bad enough, but when you feed it with a Vortec supercharger, you get the baddest boy on the block. Just ask Rayce.

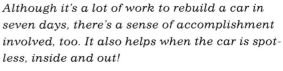

What are friends for? In the case of Rayce's good buddy Mike, they're good for helping string you out for a week while, unbeknownst to you, your car gets overhauled.

What's an overhauled car without a set of Chip Foose wheels? The five-spoke billet aluminum wheels form the façade for a set of Baer disc brakes front and rear.

progress, she volunteered, "He thought he was cool before, riding in a bucket. He's going to be untouchable now!" Actually, Rayce was going to be hot!

But not until Rayce was put through the *Overhaulin'* grinder one more time. The reveal was near, which meant that it was time to give one final twist of the dagger in the mark's back. The plan was to return to the scene of the "crime," which was a random alley where Officer McKay, aka Chris Jacobs, would reveal to Rayce that he and his friend, Mike, were under arrest because they had

been fingered by an eyewitness to the "gunfight" that took place in this very alley several nights before. The eyewitness? A homeless man who, beneath the applied grime and makeup, was none other than Chip Foose.

Officer McKay pressed the situation as far as he could, even to the extent of reading Mike and Rayce their Miranda rights. Rayce was fuming, but before the smoke could clear, Chris revealed to the mark that he had been burned by Chip Foose and his A-Team.

At one point in this episode co-host Chris Jacobs referred to Rayce's Monte Carlo as a "hunk of junk." Maybe now it's time for young Christopher to eat those words!

THE A-TEAM

Wanted: Hard-Working automotive specialist willing to work long hours for no pay

If it's true that the best things in life are free, then members of the A-Team have experienced the finest that the automotive world has to offer. Consider: they spend an entire week of their lives in an automotive shop, hunkered over a vehicle that belongs to a complete stranger, getting little rest or sleep in the process, and snatching meals or snacks when time allows. And they do all of this for no compensation other than the expression on the Mark's face at the time of the reveal.

"We're not short of people to volunteer and put in their time to work for a week, and do so with little sleep," says *Overhaulin'* show producer Bud Brutsman, with more than a slight tone of amusement, because he knows that many automotive fabricators and specialists consider it an honor to be on the A-Team. Need proof? Visit the *Overhaulin'* website where there's a special link for qualified people to sign up to be on the A-Team. Volunteers had better be good at what they do because, like Bud says, there's never a shortage.

Adds Chip Foose, "We have a waiting list of people wanting to be on the A-Team.

They know that it's a great opportunity to spend some time in the shop with experienced people who they'll learn from. The show has become a place for fabricators, painters, and other specialists to hone their skills by working with other people who have many of the same talents." Indeed, one episode included three rather seasoned volunteers who, together, had spent 196 years in the business. That's 65 years each, with one year to spare (vacation time . . .)!

Just how much sleep do the team members get during the course of a typical overhaul? According to Veronica Torres, the show's supervising producer, "sometimes less than fifty hours for the week—sometimes seven hours a night," being quick to add, "but on Day 7, sometimes no sleep at all!"

Regardless of the long days, the hectic work schedule, and the rationed hours (or minutes) of sleep, being on the A-Team is an experience few members will ever forget. As Bryan Fuller, who was among the show's first A-Team members, said, "It was a lot of work, but it also was very rewarding. I'm glad I was a part of it during the show's first season."

The A-Team from the Double Haulin' episode had to double-time it–they had two vehicles to overhaul for twin sisters Chelsea and Lindsay Cates.

'65 MUSTANG FASTBACK
Mark Griep

Mark the Mark

When is a Mark a mark? When he's Mark Griep, and his rust-bucket 1965 Mustang has been marked by Chip Foose to be overhauled. Our mark for this episode inherited the car from his late father in the 1980s, and despite oxidation that had gnawed away at the 'Stang's sheet metal and floor, Mark the mark vowed he'd never let the car leave the Griep family's grip. Chip and the A-Team, with the help of Mark's wife, Beth, and daughter Chelsea, made that possible during the seven-day filming for this episode.

Sales success aside, Ford's original Mustang deserves its landmark status in automotive history simply because it looks so cool. That legacy especially applies to the Fastback model, a car that automotive legend Carroll Shelby used as a platform for the venerable Ford-Shelby GT350 racer.

But history lessons in automotive sales, speed, and styling weren't on the minds of *Overhaulin'* crew members Chip Foose and Chris Jacobs the day they liberated Mark Griep's rusting 1965 Mustang Fastback from his driveway. Their mission was to save a car. They couldn't completely set the car free, though, until they finished its overhaul at Chicane Sport Tuning's shop in nearby Torrance, California. And while Chip and Chris played midnight auto in broad daylight, heisting the car and its parts from the backyard, Courtney Hansen posed as

This is what greeted upholstery expert Melanie Morimoto of MotoStyle—an interior full of cobwebs, missing parts, and, uh, rust, of course. She managed to salvage the seats.

Chelsea

"My dad went to both his proms—one with my mom—in the car," said Mark Griep's daughter, 16-year-old Chelsea. "My dad is into perfection," she added, "and I would really love to see him have a perfect car!" Chelsea's wish was granted, too, thanks to Chip Foose and the *Overhaulin'* A-Team, who called in a host of markers to make the Mustang's makeover possible.

Chip Foose's A-Team takes their overhauls very seriously. Mark Griep's Mustang was completely disassembled so that every nook and cranny could be treated before any paint was applied.

Melanie Morimoto came out of retirement to upholster the 'Stang's interior. She decided to maintain the classic Mustang's character, giving it a 1960s style.

Chip drew upon styling cues found in the classic Ford-Shelby GT350. The car he sketched was reminiscent of the cars Carroll Shelby built 40 years ago.

The crew from M2 Collision worked inside and out to bring the car's body back to perfection. And to think, the A-Team had only seven days to bring this rust-bucket to its new-found glory.

an eager tennis student taking lessons from Mark, a professional tennis instructor in his own right. Her job was to keep our mark preoccupied at the most crucial moment during the seven-day fix. The heist was complete and the prank was on.

Something else was on that the A-Team hadn't considered—there was enough rust on the old Mustang to coat a tramp steamer. As the A-Team exposed the pony car's skin during its deconstruction, they found more and more oxidized panels needing replacement. "I'm praying to the rust

gods," said a rather mournful Chip during the car's teardown. Added Chris, Chip's partner in crime, "This car is jack." Hmm, Mr. Foose and Mr. Jacobs, maybe crime *doesn't* pay.

There would be no payday for anybody, though, unless the A-Team got cracking. And so, taking their love for the game to greater heights, Joe Gosinski, Bryan Fuller, Kevin Byrd, Greg Coleman, Shane Boulay, Melanie Morimoto, and Craig Chaffers took to the *Overhaulin'* set to bring tennis instructor Mark Griep's "Rustang" back to life. Before they began, there was one

Top Left: This overhaul called for a complete front clip facelift. Memory Lane supplied the replacement section, and the A-Team and M2 Collision made the fit look as though it came from the Ford factory.

Top Right: The "Shelbyized" paint job complete, the car was rolled back into the shop to have its chassis aligned for the new suspension before the Ford Racing 450-horsepower V-8 was lowered into place.

Bottom Right: It's a flurry of activity as the time nears for the car's reveal. The front suspension proved especially difficult to align on Mark Griep's Mustang, but the Maier Racing crew solved the problem in time.

Bottom Left: It took Jeff Jeperson of Classy Cars Detailing many man-hours to rub out the metallic-blue and white paint job. These were the basic team colors used by American-made cars for international competition in the 1950s and 1960s.

more addition to the team—Chip's father and ace fabricator, Sam Foose, volunteered to serve as well.

With the heist successfully completed, and the A-Team elbow-deep removing the car's rust, it was time for the prank to begin. Chris assumed his usual place at the telephone, playing the role of Officer McKay who would reassure Mark that the local police department was doing everything in its power to catch the thieves who stole the car. Said a grateful Mark to Officer McKay: "Thank God there are guys like you around." The score at this point in the match: love-15 in favor of Officer McKay.

There's no question that the Ford Racing V-8 engine belongs in this car. The crate engine slipped right into place, but there was still a question about clearance for the big four-barrel carb. It fit.

Meanwhile, the Mustang was proving more stubborn than expected. "This car is a rotting animal," said one team member, and added another: "Rusted all the way through. Not good." Their comments were backed by Chip, who said, "We've got some serious rust to consider here." The only positive note came from Sam: "Chip, whoever was working on this car knew what they were doing; they quit!"

But the A-Team wasn't going to forfeit this match, ripping into the car until the rust bucket turned into a bust bucket. The net effect: The road to recovery came into view, and morale momentarily jumped off the meter when members from Ford Racing showed up with a new 450-horsepower V-8 to replace the original straight six. A G-Force transmission and fresh 8-inch rear end completed the new drivetrain.

Buoyed by the turn of events, the A-Team forged ahead, removing the

One final prank before the reveal: Officer McKay (back to the camera) makes a "suspect," actually Chip Foose in the red shirt, stand up to be identified by Mark the mark.

Here's how you overhaul a classic interior—in this case for a 1965 Ford Mustang—while retaining its original character. The sport steering wheel and competition-style dash look period-perfect for this car.

The interior's stitch panels have a unique pattern, yet the style of mirrors that are from the 1960s. Many of the replacement parts came from Year One and Summit Racing.

car's front clip to make room for a new section that Memory Lane was to deliver by the end of Day 2. This prompted the second comment from father Sam: "I told you that you stole the wrong car, Chip." The younger Foose only smiled.

Chris put on a more serious face when, as Officer McKay, he called to badger Mark the mark some more. During the phone conversation, Mark lamented that his car was probably lost forever. After hanging up, Chris said to the camera: "We keep picking these people with these sad stories, and it almost gets to me. Almost."

The following day, Mark almost caught our pranksters, too, when he spotted the tow truck and pickup truck that were used in the original

heist cruise past his house. This was the A-Team's way of playing with Mark's paranoia, and it only heightened the drama for him and the viewers.

Cut to fabricator Bryan Fuller working on the car in the shop: "It's never ending. There's more rust. It's never going to stop!" Then, on a more serious note, he explained how the A-Team was going to restyle the bumpers and front valance to give the car a tighter look. Chip also revealed that the paint job would include the patented Shelby GT350 center stripes, thus playing on the Fastback's performance heritage even more. The issue of rust was a thing of the past when the A-Team rolled the car into M2 Collision's paint booth for a

new coat of Ford metallic blue paint with white stripes.

And while the M2 crew worked their magic, Melanie Morimoto of MotoStyle stitched new upholstery onto the car's classic bucket seats. Underneath the car, the Maier Racing boys fiddled with the new suspension until all four corners were set. Then, with Mustang Joe and two of Ford Racing's engine technicians feverishly working to get the new engine to fire to life, it was nearing time for the reveal—which also meant one final opportunity to toy with Mark's mind.

Officer McKay asked Mark to come to the chop shop where his "stolen" car had been recovered. He asked Mark if he recognized any of the thieves, among them one Chip Foose, that had been "apprehended." Mark couldn't, which meant the prank was over. It was time to reveal the car.

Mark was dutifully introduced to his new car, and his first impression was that the Mustang had been, in his words, "Shelbyized," which was an apt description because the rebuilt Fastback had all the elements of the historic Shelby GT350. Game, set, and match.

'70 PONTIAC GTO
Lance Armstrong

Lance Armstrong

The Tour de France is the Super Bowl of bicycling, and nobody has even come close to matching Lance Armstrong's seven titles. But seven wins in the most grueling bicycle ride on this planet pales when compared to Lance's victory over cancer. That never-say-quit attitude on the track and in the clinic has served as inspiration to countless cancer patients around the world. As College said about his friend, "Lance has a whole new group of fans."

The number-one bicyclist in the world also happens to be a car guy. Lance Armstrong, who for seven years running, er, pedaling, established himself as perhaps the greatest bicycle racer in history by winning seven straight Tour de France events, also has a keen affection for cars. He especially favors the Pontiac GTO, which is recognized as America's first muscle car.

As a special birthday present, singer Sheryl Crow wanted to surprise Lance with a 1970 GTO convertible that he could restore. Unfortunately, before she gave him the keys, the media found out about the car and leaked the story. The surprise had been spoiled. But that was going to change. Chip Foose and the A-Team got wind of what happened, and decided to surprise Lance in another way—they'd overhaul his car, giving that Goat a kick like it never had before. Episode 209 was underway, taking place in Lance's hometown of Austin, Texas.

The first step was to rustle the car away from its owner, the guy *Overhaulin'* cohost Courtney Hansen

Sheryl Crow

It's been said that music is the universal language, which makes Sheryl Crow a universal linguist. Her best-selling songs include "All I Wanna Do," "My Favorite Mistake," and "Leaving Las Vegas," among others. And for one particular week she had Lance Armstrong singing the blues about his stolen Pontiac GTO. But after the reveal, he changed his tune, and it was one of thanks and gratitude to Sheryl, Chip Foose, and the A-Team.

When it's time for Lance to put the pedal to the metal in his new ride, he'll be joined by some great tunes. Kicker provided the audio addition to this cool convertible.

As with many of the cars that get overhauled on the program, Lance Armstrong's 1970 GTO had more rust than originally suspected. This required additional time to eradicate.

The Tour de Overhaul was a success, Lance and Sheryl are joined by the A-Team for a final photo. Like the mark, Chip Foose's A-Team performed like champions to finish the car in time.

respectfully referred to as "Bike Boy." The solution was to enlist the help of Lance's long-time friend John "College" Korioth, who volunteered to take the car to a reputable shop for what Lance understood to be routine service. But wouldn't you know, some "thieves" stole the car from the shop where College dropped it off the day before. Those thieves were Chip Foose and College himself.

Chip asked College as they casually drove away the car, top down, for its seven-day overhaul, "How do you like being a car thief?" Replied College, "I love it."

Chip and College delivered the GTO to Colvin's Automotive, where the A-Team had assembled for the overhaul. Shop owner K. C. Colvin had volunteered the use of his shop for the project. Joining him and Chip were Craig Chaffers, Steve Chappo, Roy Piqford, Tony Genty of Original Parts Group, Jeff "Grumpy" Farina, Jorge Lopez, Richard Wood, and Jim Griffin. Before the car's deconstruction began, Chip gathered everybody to ceremoniously hand out yellow wristbands in honor of Lance's successful fight against cancer a few years ago. "We're going to *band* together," he said, then work commenced at a fever pitch. "Livestrong" was their slogan.

When the A-Team stripped the paint, they encountered rust and corrosion in the sheet metal. The

To the untrained eye there's not much that differentiates this dash from the original. However, the instrument insert, steering wheel, in-dash air conditioner controls, and padding are all new.

Lance Armstrong insists on black-on-black for his cars, so Chip Foose asked Jim Griffin to come up with a black leather interior that was striking in appearance.

bare body was taken to Sandblasters for media blasting to reveal the full extent of its rot.

Meanwhile, Sheryl stopped by for a quick look and to help Chip decide on some of the detail work that would go into the car. She explained that Lance loved black cars; no other color would do. A momentary hush fell over the A-Team because every car guy knows that black paint will show even the smallest imperfection in the body's sheet metal.

But Sheryl's words didn't faze Chip, who began sketching the concept on paper. When finished, a

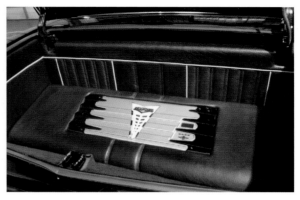

Leaving no detail untouched, Chip Foose asked the A-Team to disassemble the new engine for paint. Part of the request focused on lettering "Livestrong" on the valve covers.

The heartbeat of Kicker's audio system is found in the trunk. Jim Griffin worked wonders to stitch the black Keystone leather throughout the trunk and four-seat interior.

black-on-black rendition of what Chip envisioned for the 1970 GTO convertible covered the page. "What we want to do," Chip said, "is build Lance's dream car." Day 1 was in the books, and there was no backpedaling now. The A-Team had to fulfill Chip's vision.

Day 2 brought a few more surprises, plus a new engine from Butler Performance. Then Chip pitched another curveball: He told the A-Team to disassemble the engine so they could paint the block, cylinder heads, manifold, and water pump. Plans also called for inscribing the word "Livestrong" on the two valve covers.

Meanwhile John Hotchkis of Hotchkis Performance came to

inspect the car's suspension. He decided to install all-new components, plus beef up the underpinnings with anti-sway bars, heavy-duty shock absorbers and springs, and hefty Baer disc brakes. Hotchkis was giving Lance's car the *tour de force* treatment.

It was also time to give Lance the *tour de runaround*. It was prank time, and Chris Jacobs checked in as Paul Ramonofsky, the police officer making the initial theft report with the car's owner, Lance Armstrong. "Mr. Armstrong," he said when wrapping up the interview, "my father, Chip, is a huge, huge fan of yours. Could you sign this?" he asked, handing Lance the famous photograph showing the bicyclist with his arms raised

high, six fingers spread to celebrate Tour de France win number six. While Lance signed the picture, Chris said he was confident that Lance could win his sixth Tour de France. A little miffed, Lance politely pointed out that he had already won six; that was why the photograph showed him holding up six fingers. "Oh," replied Chris, feigning embarrassment, "I thought you were saying, 'I'm number one—I've won five!'" It was an A-Team performance that also helped keep Lance guessing—about his car and about the people entrusted to recover it.

There was no faking or feigning the GTO's overhaul, though. The Goat received its new coat of black paint by Roy Piqford's crew at Roy's Body Shop, while Jim Griffin of Griffin Interiors was busy stitching the black cowhide for the interior. For cruisin' tunes, a new Kicker sound system was installed, and just to make sure Lance would be cool at all times in his car, the guys from nearby Vintage Air installed a new air conditioning unit. Add a set of Foose Design wheels with BFGoodrich rubber, and a specially made bicycle rack, and we've got one stylin' convertible.

Time for the reveal, and Lance showed up at the
alleged chop shop to identify the recovered car. But first,
one more prank. Officer Ramonofsky pulled out a video-
tape of his rock band, and asked Lance if he might pass it
on to Sheryl Crow to check out. This time, Lance tried to
ignore the starstruck police officer's behavior entirely.

But Chris was for real, and so were the A-Team and
the overhauled 1970 GTO that they presented to Lance.
The overhaul complete, Lance Armstrong, the world's
number-one bicyclist who was destined to win an unprece-
dented seven Tour de France titles, was speechless. "I
don't think I've ever been fooled like this in my life," he
said, thanking each and every A-Team member.

Livestrong and prosper, Lance. And enjoy your Goat!

'62 CHEVROLET BEL AIR

Glenn Atkins

Glenn Atkins

By day, Glenn works with disabled pre-school children, and at night he's a full-time father to twin toddler boys. As you might guess, this busy schedule leaves Glenn little time to tinker with his fixer-upper car at night, which, as it turned out, made Glenn the perfect mark for this episode.

Don't ever think that you can outwit the A-Team. Just ask Glenn Atkins, who, as a regular *Overhaulin'* viewer, felt that should the occasion ever arise with his rusted and busted 1962 Chevrolet Bel Air two-door sedan, he would be too smart and sharp-eyed to be fooled by the pranks and shenanigans that Chip Foose's corps of car guys plays on their unwitting marks. Said Glenn on Day 7 when the *Overhaulin'* crew revealed his restored Chevy, "I didn't think they could ever fool me."

Indeed, Glenn *had* been fooled, and in his words he was, well, speechless. "I'm speechless," he said, as he examined the new shiny black car that sat regally before him on California Performance Transmission's shop floor in Huntington Beach, California, where the overhaul took place. "I can't believe it," he uttered, amazed that his ugly duckling had been transformed into a beautiful swan. Believe it, Glenn, because as *Overhaulin'* co-host Courtney Hansen said at the beginning of the episode,

Jennifer Atkins, wife

Jennifer describes her husband, Glenn, as a "doer and a giver," a person who unselfishly gives his time to others. Jennifer continues: "Around others, Glenn takes himself seriously . . . . He does stress out because he always has a lot on his plate with work, school, favors for others, and personal time." The *Overhaulin'* team added to Glenn's stress for seven days, but managed to relieve it when they revealed his finished car on Day 7.

"the owner gets tricked and the car gets tricked out." Glenn was clearly tricked, and his beater car certainly got tricked out.

So just exactly how did the A-Team trick Glenn, anyway? The prank began with a flyer left on his windshield from a fictitious music company requesting the use of Glenn's classic car for a promotional video. Glenn responded, agreeing to rent them his old Chevy for a couple days. What could it hurt, he reasoned? The additional money would come in handy.

But while Glenn's mind was busy exploring ways he would spend his new windfall, the A-Team was busy giving his car its new look. The facelift began none too soon, because the Chevy's sheet metal revealed more than a few rust holes. In Courtney's words, "Holy moly, there are a whole lot of holes here." The oxidation overdose was compounded by a trunk lid that

The Chevy's chrome and stainless-steel trim was in satisfactory condition when the old clunker rolled in—backwards, because only the reverse gear worked— to the shop for its overhaul.

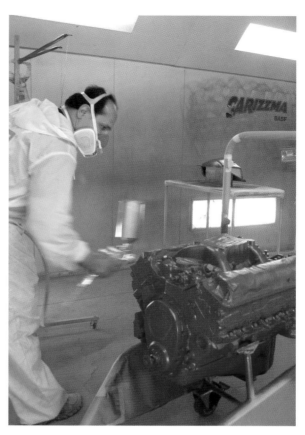

refused to open and close properly because the car had been rear-ended heavily sometime between 1962 and the beginning of the overhaul.

None of that deterred Chip and his crew, which was led by Art Carr, whose shop the A-Team called home for the week. The two legends—Art, the master transmission builder, and Chip, the all-around fabricator and designer—were joined by Craig Chaffers, Shane Boulay, Chris Bassett, Jeff Binder, Jeremy Hayter, Craig "Captain" Watts, Brian Hohman, and James Brutsman. Mitch Lanzini's shop took on the bodywork and paint, and Ray Miller gathered needle and thread to stitch the car's bright red upholstery. Guaranty Chevrolet shipped a new 350 crate motor to replace the car's original, somewhat tired six-cylinder engine, and California Performance Transmission supplied an overdrive

Left: A victim of more than one rear-end fender-bender, the A-Team spent a lot of time fixing the Chevy's hindquarters. Here Chip Foose works from the inside out to get things straight.

Right: After the A-Team taped and prepped the new engine, Mitch Lanzini rolled the block into his spray booth to apply bright red paint. The interior was to receive the same color.

automatic transmission to replace the car's dated three-speed manual box. Hotchkis brought over all-new underpinnings for the chassis, Baer brakes were posted at all four corners, and the Foose retro-styled five-spoke wheels were wrapped with BFGoodrich rubber. A MagnaFlow exhaust system offered a deep, but mellow, exhaust note. To make all this happen, the A-Team merely had to spend the remaining six days and nights assembling the car. Meanwhile, Chris Jacobs was assigned the task of keeping Glenn guessing about his car's whereabouts. To do that, Chris assumed the role of John McDermott, the alleged spokesman for the even more alleged music video production company.

McDermott began the prank with a phone call to Glenn, explaining that the film crew had finished and was set to return the car to him the following day. Right on schedule, a tow truck showed up the next morn-

Foose Design five-spoke wheels help carry the traditional styling theme to all four corners. Baer brakes with drilled rotors are stylish reminders that this car boasts current technology, too.

Guaranty Chevrolet supplied the 350 crate engine. The A-Team took it from there, dressing it with a handful of hot rod parts from Summit Racing's inventory of cool parts.

ing, but with the wrong car on its towbed. Glenn called McDermott to explain his displeasure. McDermott remained evasive about the situation, causing Glenn to lose his patience. "Let me speak slowly so you can understand me," said a somewhat agitated Glenn, "they dropped off *the wrong car*." McDermott feigned understanding and sympathy, but that was the last Glenn would hear from him. McDermott—actually Chris Jacobs—stirred up the hornet's nest even more, evading Glenn's ensuing phone calls for the remaining few days. Only the reveal could save Glenn's patience now.

After seven days of round-the-clock work, the overhaul was finished in time for the reveal. The A-Team celebrates with this episode's mark, Glenn Atkins, standing in front for the ceremonial signoff.

Subtle changes to the front bumper help clean up the Chevy's overall lines. As the A-Team points out time and again, sometimes it's the attention to the little details that makes the big difference.

There were problems back at the shop, though. Day 7 had arrived, and with the reveal scheduled for that afternoon, the new engine refused to start, despite reassurances from Jeff that the small-block V-8 would fire the "first time." The problem was traced to a faulty starter, and after a quick trip to the local parts house for a replacement, the A-Team completed the R&R in minutes. True to Jeff's words, the engine indeed fired up on the first try.

Ray completed his razzle-dazzle job on the interior, even placing the two custom-trimmed Simpson child restraint seats in the back so that

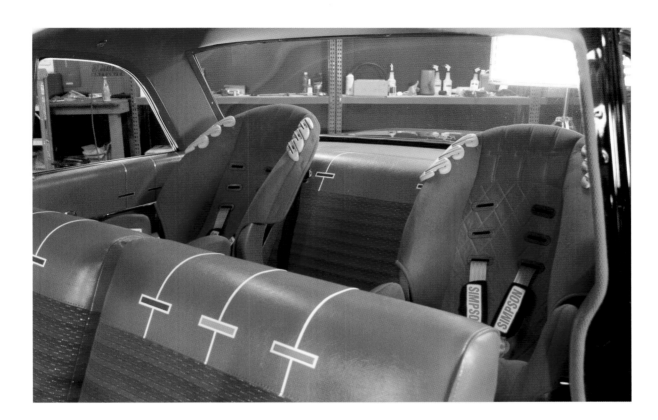

This is a family car, first and foremost, which explains the two customized Simpson baby seats that the A-Team made sure were included in the all-red interior.

Black cars with red interiors have always been popular, and this one will no doubt be a hit with people for years to come. Retaining the front bench seats underscores that this is a family car.

Glenn's twin boys would feel right at home in the overhauled car. And only yards away on the other side of the shop door stood Glenn with a police officer who had summoned him to identify his car and the thief who stole it. The accused thief was escorted out the door to face Glenn, and immediately our unsuspecting mark recognized him to be Chip Foose. "Oh, no," exclaimed Glenn, "I've been overhauled!"

Yes, Glenn, you—or more specifically, your car—had been overhauled, "tricked out," as Courtney says. As for you, well, you were tricked. Notch up another episode in favor of the A-Team.

The overhaul complete, Glenn's Chevy sits on the shop floor at California Performance Transmission, where it awaits the reveal. The car's timeless traditional lines reveal themselves well at this angle.

'52 GMC PICKUP TRUCK
John Park

John Park

John (shown with his mother at the reveal) had plans to restore his 1952 GMC pickup truck after he finished his education to become a chiropractor. After the A-Team delivered the overhauled truck to John, and after his "thank you," he offered free chiropractic care to all the A-Team members. Now that's what we call a real payback.

T he A-Team gave true meaning to the term "charity case" when they targeted John Park's distressed 1952 GMC pickup truck for its overhaul. The caper that led to the heist of John's pickup hinged on making him believe that a local charity organization accepted his beater truck as a tax-deductible donation.

The heist took place in broad daylight after John left for work. The truck sat unattended, yet supposedly safe, in his housing complex's gated and locked parking lot. But with the help of John's brother-in-law, Brian Cruz, to open the gate, the A-Team loaded the old Jimmy pickup on the back of Century Towing's tow truck and hauled it away. The crew left a tax receipt on John's front door that also thanked him for his charitable donation.

As the A-Team embarked on the deconstruction process, co-host Courtney Hansen said, "This truck

All the body work would be pointless if the truck didn't have a low stance, so Chip directed the A-Team to cut and reposition the frame rails to give John's truck the proper stance.

Brian Cruz

Like the rest of John's family, brother-in-law Brian not only wanted to see the GMC pickup finished, he was tired of looking at its primer finish. Brian's solution was to contact the A-Team and volunteer his brother-in-law's Jimmy truck for an overhaul. When it was time for the heist, Brian supplied the keys to the truck for a smooth getaway. The "theft" complete, Brian now qualifies as John's brother-in-outlaw.

looks like it needs a giant seven-day hug." It was going to get more than just a hug. Added co-host Chris Jacobs, "As Foose likes to say—'let's get rid of the ugly.'" One by one, the parts were removed, as Courtney put it, to be "revived, recycled, and just plain rejuvenated."

Getting rid of the ugly also meant removing years of old Bondo and the original lead body filler applied by General Motors when the truck was built in 1952. By now, Chip Foose had a vision of what the finished truck would look like, prompting him to give the order: "Now we start cutting and pasting." In Foose-speak that means reshaping the body.

Most of the initial work was focused on the front where Chip wanted to give the truck its own character. He cut out the headlight buckets, replacing them with sections that he pirated from a 1956 Chevrolet Bel Air. After he "pasted" them into place, the team cut and shaped a 1955 Chevrolet front bumper and grille section to fit. The transformation gave viewers a firsthand look at how a real show car is created.

Chip Foose deemed the truck's front end (top) unacceptable. What he conceived with the A-Team's help is a front (bottom) that has all the style and flavor of a full-blown show truck.

While Foose fiddled with the fenders, other team members formed and smoothed a new firewall, and tended to the various holes and rust spots on the body. The truck was beginning to take on a new personality. But it wasn't enough for Chip, who directed his attention to the Jimmy's stance. Simply, as it sat now, this custom truck wasn't going to sit low enough for Chip's liking. Solution: cut and raise the frame's rear section. That also meant relocating the front suspension's hangers so the

Chip Foose, with help from Scratch (left), slides a chrome trimpiece onto the hood of the 1952 GMC.

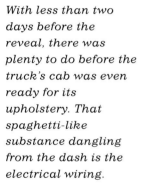

With less than two days before the reveal, there was plenty to do before the truck's cab was even ready for its upholstery. That spaghetti-like substance dangling from the dash is the electrical wiring.

truck sat level. It was a job that normally required many days, even weeks, but the A-Team completed it in less than two days. Even so, the crew was behind schedule. Said Craig Chaffers, "Since we're two days behind, we can't have any hangups now."

Chris couldn't have any hangups, either, as he began his phone pranks with John. Chris posed as Melvin Everett, a representative from the charity organization that acquired John's truck. He politely thanked John for the donation, but our mark didn't see it that way: "I want my truck back," he told Everett. A little blundering and fumbling with words on Everett's part left John wondering who, exactly, he was dealing with. He would find out in a few more days, but only after Chris kept him in the pressure cooker. Chris's next call would be as Detective Casavetes, who would later enlist John to participate in the sting that would catch the thieves who stole his truck and, hopefully, get the pickup back to its rightful owner.

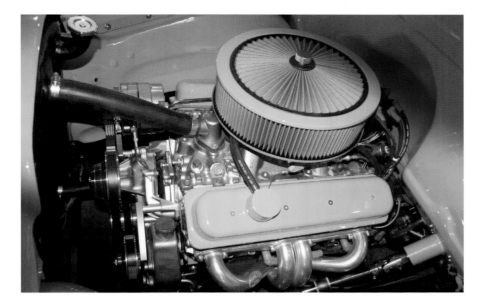

The engine tested fine on the break-in stand, and after it received some touch-up paint here and there, the A-Team slid it into place. The truck's fire-wall was extensively modified to fit the engine.

The high-performance 383-cubic-inch small-block Chevy engine develops 350 horse-power and 450 ft-lb of torque at the crank. The A-Team tested the engine on an engine stand before installation.

Before John was to see his truck again, there was plenty of work to be done. The modified frame was sent to the powder-coater for finishing, and Caliber Collision had a small army of workers—25 to be precise—waiting at their shop for the body sections to be delivered so they could finish prepping them for paint. It was a monumental task, and everywhere in the Caliber shop men were grinding, filling, and block-sanding body parts from one single truck—John's 1952 Jimmy.

Stitchcraft Interiors worked overtime to trim the truck's cab and OPG bucket seats with matching leather upholstery. The door panels have traditional-style tuck-and-roll inserts.

A classic three-spoke steering wheel is perched atop the Flaming Rivers column. Round vintage-style gauges and a reconditioned center insert help retain the truck's old-style charm.

Chip selected a rather bold yellow, what he calls Butterscortch, for the paint. Fortunately there were no graphics or multi-hues to slow the process, and with about a day remaining, the Caliber crew returned the body for assembly. The home stretch saw the 383-cubic-inch Chevrolet small-block engine lowered into place, and the drivetrain coupled together.

Stitchcraft Interiors tackled the cab, trimming it with leather to match the Butterscortch paint, and Brothers Truck Parts delivered a truckload of components to finish out the project, including new wood slats and aluminum trim strips for the bed. When the A-Team was finished, John's truck looked good enough to be entered in a car show.

But its first showing would be to John who, by now, was convinced that Detective Casavetes was hot on the trail of an unsuspecting car-theft ring. John even volunteered to be wired for listening devices to help nab

the thieves. He was sent to the chop shop's back door where he knocked and was greeted by various A-Team members posing as car thieves. Each time, he was told to wait outside while the thieves conferred with one another inside the shop.

Finally Courtney walked up, posing as another victim. She innocently said to John, "Wouldn't it be funny if we were on the program called *Overhaulin'*, where they overhaul your car in a week?" End of prank, and beginning of the reveal. John was completely fooled, and he graciously accepted his fate, and his truck.

If it's true that charity begins at home, then Chip Foose's A-Team is right at home overhauling cars and trucks like John's GMC pickup. This episode was truly a charity case for the ages.

'65 FORD PICKUP TRUCK
John deAlva

John deAlva

As a car guy, John deAlva has been conditioned to stand by his ride, no matter what. As a Navy Seal, he has been trained, under all conditions, to stand his ground. And that's exactly what he did for seven days, refusing to give in to the pitiful settlement offer that the insurance company was willing to pay for his stolen truck. His conviction paid off, and he was treated to one ship-shape pickup truck. Viewers also saw John stand behind his long-lost comrade, Mitch, whose memory he dedicated this overhaul to.

Mention the words "Navy Seals" to anybody familiar with today's U.S. Armed Forces, and they'll envision stealthy, behind-the-lines commandos who can adapt to practically any situation. These guys are tough and resourceful, and are trained to cope under all conditions. All conditions, that is, unless they're dealing with the ever-industrious A-Team.

And it was at the beginning of *Overhaulin's* third season that the A-Team went into action, going head-to-head with America's elite Special Forces to overhaul former Seal John deAlva's 1965 Ford F-100 pickup truck. Realizing that the best way to fight fire is with fire, the A-Team bolstered their firepower with five current and former members of the elite Navy Seals team. Reporting for duty to Commander Chip Foose were Kelly Zarrabi, Matthew Roberts, Mark Stover, Juan Jauregui, and Jon Savage. The Seals were joined by A-Team veterans Roger Willis, Craig Chaffers, Shane Boulay, Andreas Somogyi, and Shawn Hengstebeck. Additional logistical support

▶ INSIDER

Angela deAlva

It's been said that behind every successful man is a woman. If John doesn't owe his success as a Navy Seal to his wife Angela, then he certainly is indebted to her for his overhauled Ford pickup truck. Angela not only arranged for the A-Team to overhaul John's ride, but she managed to help keep him thinking that his truck had not only been stolen, but was worth more than the settlement figure the insurance company had offered him.

▶ ACCOMPLICE

Paul Danberger

If you're a diehard car guy, it's important to have a reputable repair shop where you can take your ride when it needs some serious service or repair work. John calls on Paul's Car Care at times to make sure his 1965 Ford pickup truck receives the attention it deserves. But for one week, shop owner Paul Danberger managed to get John's attention when he helped the A-Team with this overhaul.

The interior reported for duty in so-so condition (left). But that wasn't good enough for the A-Team, so with a little help from Bill Dunn Interiors and J&G Audio the cab became a lean, mean sitting machine.

You may know Roush Racing for its success on the NASCAR circuit, but they also make aftermarket engines. This polished and painted beauty carries the Roush Racing logo.

You don't give a former Navy Seal's truck just an ordinary engine, so Chip Foose called the troops at Roush Racing for one of their race-ready V-8s. Here Chip inspects the frame for clearance.

was provided by Rod Olmsted (engine); Mark Banuelos (National Parts Depot); Hector and the gang from Bill Dunn Interiors; J&G Audio technicians; and the body and paint crew from Anaheim Hills Auto Body.

Ground zero for the overhaul was Paul's Car Care, where John left his truck for a new rear bumper to be installed. Paul Danberger was recruited as an accomplice, along with John's wife, Angela, to make sure that John delivered the truck on time. After all, the A-Team had a mission to accomplish, and its success hinged on keeping to a tight schedule. Almost immediately after John left Paul's shop, the A-Team sprung into action, driving the truck to a nearby shop for its overhaul. The following day, Paul called John to give him the bad news: His truck was lost in action—it had been "stolen."

All the frame cross-members were replaced or modified for the new Roush Racing engine and Art Carr transmission. Said Chip, "Basically all we're saving from the original frame are the frame rails."

The crew at Anaheim Hills Auto Body completed the paint job just in time to set the body onto the rebuilt chassis. Hard to believe that in less than a day this truck will be back on the road!

The truck's theft was bad enough for John, but intelligence reports from the A-Team's spies confirmed that the Ford also had sentimental value to him. It embodied the spirit of his deceased friend, Mitch. John and Mitch had been boyhood buddies, and when they were young men, Mitch bought a new Firebird, presenting John with his old 1965 Ford F-100 so they both had wheels. To show his gratitude, John vowed that one day he'd restore the aging truck. But duty and honor to his country came first, and when John joined the Navy Seals he had to part with the truck. Sadly, in 1996 Mitch passed away unexpectedly, but the following year John was in a position to buy a replacement 1965 Ford pickup; one day, he promised himself, he'd restore the truck in Mitch's memory. The restoration would have to wait, though, because most of John's time and energy was spent doing what Navy Seals are trained to do. After he resigned from the military, his time on the home front was devoted to raising his three boys with wife, Angela. John would pick up where he left off with the truck only when the time was right.

John (plain T-shirt) stands with five of his former Navy Seal comrades who actually helped with this overhaul. They're just as close in the shop as they are out on the field of action.

Chip Foose deemed the time right for Episode 308, and what the A-Team dismantled was a rather rust-free 1965 Ford pickup. That didn't mean it was going to be an easy rebuild—as with all overhauls, Chip Foose sought perfection for this truck. Among the hurdles were frame clearance for the Roush Racing engine and steering box, and the sheet metal's finish—it needed to be perfect. Moreover, Chip wanted to make sure the truck embodied the spirit of John's friend Mitch. A subtle touch that Chip worked into the design was to paint Mitch's name on the glove-box door. After viewing Chip's artist renderings of what the truck would become, Angela said with emotion,

"This is the truck that's made for John." Chip was on target. Now it was time for the A-Team to execute the battle plan.

While the A-Team worked toward their goal, Chris Jacobs covered their six, posing as an insurance claims adjuster. A phone call to John led to a proposed cash settlement for the truck. John said that it was actually irreplaceable, but Chris finally offered $2,500. "I know what you're doing, and it's completely arbitrary," said John moments before hanging up. Chris said to the *Overhaulin'* camera: "This guy's a Navy Seal and he wants to kill me." Chris had his mark exactly where he wanted him.

Chip Foose designed a set of wheels specifically for this overhaul. The wheels' five-spoke design complements the truck's classic lines. Clearly they won John's "seal" of approval.

A few more phone calls to John proved Chris right. Had this been war, Chris would have been the mark, not John. Fortunately, this was Episode 308 of the family television show *Overhaulin'*, which meant that Chris and the A-Team had to take one final jab at John before the reveal. The final act was played at Paul's shop, where Chris Jacobs eventually confronted John face-to-face. As a regular *Overhaulin'* viewer, John immediately recognized the show's co-host, and realized that he had been had. Mission accomplished, and time to show John his new truck.

In recognition of John's training as a Navy Seal, the A-Team mustered up a field first-aid kit to install on the truck. Just like the Boy Scouts of America, Seals always need to be prepared.

The reveal went smoothly, and John did what practically every *Overhaulin'* mark has done—he walked around the truck in awe, amazed that the entire rebuild took less than a week to complete. When he saw Mitch's name on the glove box he stopped in his tracks. "You've got Mitch's name in there," he said quietly. Thanks in large part to the A-Team, John's promise had been kept.

Remarked John when the reveal was complete: "I'll drive it with pride, thinking of all the hard work you [the A-Team] put into it, and to the men and women serving overseas." Consider this *Overhaulin'* episode signed, *sealed*, and delivered.

John's truck got a complete facelift during the overhaul. Simply by retaining the stock components, the A-Team's resourcefulness was enough to give the truck a completely new look.

Above: *Mitch lives on! In a tribute to John's childhood friend, Chip and the A-Team had Mitch's name striped onto the glove-box door* **Below**: *Tucked inside the box is the truck's new sound system.*

'65 CHEVROLET IMPALA
Martin Betancourt

Martin and Vanessa

Shortly before Martin and Vanessa married, the bride-to-be learned an important lesson about her future husband: He was, effectively, already married to his car, a 1965 Chevrolet Impala. The lesson came when they were making wedding plans. Why not sell the old Chevy, asked Vanessa. "Big mistake," she later told *Overhaulin'*. "I then learned that he would never sell the car." In fact, Martin explained to her that one day he hoped to restore the car. But as a devoted father and husband, Martin realized that family—not family heirlooms—comes first, so the Chevy had to wait. But Vanessa didn't, and she called *Overhaulin'* to see if Martin's Impala qualified for an episode. And the rest, as they say, is history.

Family heirlooms are not created in an instant, nor does any one family member decide what becomes a keepsake and what can be sold at the next yard sale. No, heirlooms evolve over time, and even though they are only material things, those inanimate objects eventually become part of the family. They are not to be sold, given away, or, heaven forbid, lost.

So it was when Juan Betancourt sold the family car—a 1965 Chevrolet Impala two-door hardtop that he had owned since it was new—without informing the members of his clan that a few eyebrows were raised at the dinner table when he broke the news. The person most vocal about the sale was Juan's son Martin. In fact, Martin did more than voice his displeasure—he went to the new owner (fortunately, a family friend) and asked if he'd annul the deal, which he did. The Betancourt household was once again a whole family unit, but the Chevy was in need of restoration, something that Martin couldn't really afford.

Like a swarm of busy bees, the A-Team attacks Martin's 1965 Chevrolet Impala. The deconstruction began after Chris Jacobs, acting as a car thief, stole the car right off the city street.

Fast forward a few years, and young Martin is now a married man with two boys, and a teacher for the local school district. He still owns the Impala, but it has no seat belts, and the car's aging 409 engine burns oil in equal proportion to gasoline. In short, it's a prime candidate for an overhaul, and one night *Overhaulin's* covert cast member, Chris Jacobs, makes the heist, driving Martin's classic Chevy to Classic Industries for its long-overdue overhaul. "What a classic car to overhaul," says Chris for the benefit of *Overhaulin's* viewers.

The A-Team agreed with Chris' assessment, and they dug into the deconstruction process like hungry piranhas tearing at a fresh piece of flesh. The kingfish, of course, is Chip Foose, who's restored his fair share of classic cars. He was joined by project manager Craig Chaffers, Roger Willis, Andreas Somogyi, Shane Boulay, Shawn Hengstebeck,

No part of the car is overlooked when the A-Team overhauls it. The deconstruction process sometimes requires that team members climb into compartments not intended for humans.

Sean Hughes, Kristine DesBiens, Chris Howe, Aaron Kaufman, Richard Rawlings, and Austin Potter. Lurking in the shadows and ready to pounce when called upon were Tom Rodriquez Sr.'s body builders at Cypress Auto; Travis Preciado and his sound crew from Al & Ed's Audio; Gary and Eddie from Protek Alarms; and Bill Dunn, who would stitch the interior. They formed quite an ensemble—"a family," as Chip likes to say—for this overhaul.

It's not a classic overhaul, though, without the prank. Since Martin was a big fan of *Overhaulin'*, he'd recognize Chris or A. J., or even Mr. Foose himself, if they went mano a mano with him, so a relatively unknown face was given the task of confronting

Chip Foose decided from the beginning that they'd retain the classic 409 engine in Martin's car. L&R was given the honor of rebuilding the big-block motor, and linked it to an SW-built automatic transmission.

If even the smallest component looks like it will disrupt the lines of the car, Chip Foose says "eliminate it." And so it was—the keyholes on the doors and trunk lid were sent to the showers.

Stripped to the bone, the classic Impala two-door hardtop body is ready to be shipped to Cypress Auto Body, where it would be prepped and given its two-tone paint job.

Martin with the news that his car had been used in an illegal smuggling operation at nearby Los Angeles Harbor. Agent Brutsman (if the name is familiar, Bud Brutsman is the show's producer, and his name was predominantly displayed on the inspector's shirt, so Martin *could* have had a clue) of the U.S. Customs Service asked mark Martin to come to the docks so he could answer some questions about his purportedly stolen car. Down at the docks, one thing led to another until Agent Brutsman all but accused our mark and his friend Mike of conspiring to

help smuggle substances of unknown origins past U.S. Customs. Our schoolteacher was getting a firsthand lesson in civics, and he didn't like it.

Meanwhile, back at Classic Industries, our school of piranhas continued chewing on the Chevy. Once they nibbled off the old paint they found portions of the body that had been repaired—rather poorly—in the past. As the A-Team completed the necessary repairs, viewers were treated to a quick lesson in how to form sheet metal by heating, shrinking, and hammering

Chip felt that painting the five-spoke wheels the same color as the stripe panels on the hood and trunk would emphasize the Impala's new hot-rod persona. Those tires are from B. F. Goodrich.

Some of Detroit's most stylish dashboards are from the 1950s and 1960s. The A-Team restored the dash using many reproduction components available from Classic Industries' inventory.

Martin is a family man, and even though the Impala now warrants hot-rod stature, it remains a family car. Given that status, the A-Team made sure there's a custom child seat for Martin's son.

ROBERTO

King for a Day

While the premise for *Ovehaulin'* is to entertain television viewers, sometimes the weeklong project addresses something much more important. In the course of overhauling Martin Betancourt's 1965 Chevy Impala, Chip Foose and the A-Team welcomed a special visitor—seven-year-old Roberto from Make-A-Wish Foundation—to the set.

Roberto's wish was to meet Chip Foose and to be on the set of *Overhaulin'*. His wish came true for two days.

"His favorite part," recalls Chip, "was when we installed the engine. He wanted to see the actual install, so we rigged a monitor so he could watch as we put the engine into the car." What the camera saw, Roberto saw.

Before Roberto left, Chip sketched and painted a Shelby Mustang for him. It is Roberto's favorite car, and the artist's rendering means even more to him because Chip signed it. "It's more than just about building cars," says Chip. "It's about building relationships." Add one more person to Chip Foose's long list of friends.

the sections into shape. These were methods handed down from metalsmiths to their sons, who passed the techniques to their sons, until the time-honored secrets found their way to the A-Team family members.

While the A-Team clan tackled the Betancourt family car, Martin's wife, Vanessa, brought the car's original owner to the shop for a peek. Juan viewed the car shortly after Cypress Auto had applied the R-M Paint black base coat, and Tom Rodriquez Sr. explained that once the clear topcoat was applied, the paint would glisten and have depth.

A half-dozen flush-fit taillights brighten up the Chevy's hind quarters. Chip retained the classic Chevy emblem on the trunk lid, but he removed the key lock and trimmed the bumper.

But that would happen only after Chip and Dennis applied the pewter-colored panel stripes on the hood and trunk lid. This car was beginning to look more and more like a hot rod.

The classic 409 engine would do more than glisten, though. The guys at L&R rebuilt it top to bottom, gifting the big-block with a six-pack of two-barrel carburetors, too. This big V-8 was going to bark to the world that it was a hot rod engine, and that

The 409 is actually the second incarnation—after the venerable 348—of Chevrolet's first big-block V-8. The intake manifold was machined to lower the six carburetors to clear the hood when shut.

was exactly what Chip had in mind. But that wouldn't happen until the A-Team figured out how to make the six carbs clear the hood. Chip found the solution on the milling machine where he fly-cut the intake manifold so the carburetors would sit lower on the engine. That "minor" technicality solved, it was time for the reveal.

Martin's friend Mike stepped in again to help with the reveal. He told Martin that "the boss" wanted his help so they could clear the car through customs. Simply, the boss showed up with a bag full of money that he wanted Martin to deliver to Agent Brutsman, and in return the Chevy would be conveniently, and quietly, released. Martin thought the whole situation was fishy, but before the prank went any further Agent Jacobs appeared, and Martin knew right away what the previous week was all about. Next stop: Classic Industries, where Martin would

see his car for the first time in a week. What greeted him was, essentially, a whole new car.

"This is what the car's supposed to look like," said an astonished Martin as he surveyed the car. "I just won the hot rod lotto, huh?" he added.

Finally, the initial excitement behind him, Martin put into perspective what the overhauled car meant to him: "This car is family," he said with emotion. Yes, Martin, it is family. And to help him celebrate his new family ride, Martin invited his father to get behind the wheel for a drive. "Just like old times," Martin said. Once again the Betancourt family had been reunited with its 1965 Chevrolet Impala.

OVERHAULIN' *ALUMNI*

Building Cars with Class

Overhauling a complete car in a week's time involves more than just splashing a fresh coat of paint on its sheet metal, mixing in some shiny chromed parts, and refurbishing the interior. When Chip Foose and the A-Team completely rebuild a car for an episode, they do just that, rebuilding everything inside and out to reflect the personality of its owner.

"The goal is to build our Mark's dream car," says Chip. Moreover, every car that's been customized by the A-Team is a car that's fully street worthy, too.

But the A-Team's focus also is to make the car striking in appearance.

"The guy off the street will look at one of these cars and say, 'Wow, that's a nice hot rod.' But the guy who's actually into hot rods will look at it and appreciate the quality of the car—the fit and finish," continues Chip.

Above all else, it's that fit and finish that Chip and the A-Team strive for, so when the car is revealed to its owner on Day 7, there's no mistaking that this is a special vehicle. "Later, when people recognize the car on the street," concludes Chip, "I want them to say, 'Oh, that's one of the cars from *Overhaulin'.*'"

The first-ever seasonal episode featured Jeff Miller's 1971 Chevrolet Chevelle that was in need of more than a few new parts. The A-Team, with the help of Original Parts Group, finished the job.

Matt Mershimer inherited this 1988 Chevrolet pickup truck from his grandfather. The A-Team transformed it into a family heirloom for this honor-roll high school student.

This 1967 Buick Skylark was handed down to Rick Garcia from his brother Robert. Acting on more than a lark, big brother also helped prank Rick during the overhaul.

Behind every good man is a woman, and behind the prank that led to the overhaul of James Rodaer's 1971 Dodge Challenger is his wife, Stephanie.

'05 DODGE MAGNUM HEMI
Joanna Young

Joanna Young

One expatriated subject of the Queen's Empire who appreciates American driving habits and cars is Joanna Young. She finds it quite proper to drive on the right side of the road, and she's rather fond of cars powered by big V-8 engines. A person would be daft to settle for anything less. And so Joanna, who currently lives among the colonists near the city of Los Angeles, drives a 2005 Dodge Magnum, one of America's modern-day muscle cars powered by a good ol' Hemi V-8.

Even though British and American motorists speak the same language, their driving habits are diametrically opposed. *They*—meaning the Brits—drive on the left side of the road, which as any red-blooded American will tell you, also happens to be the wrong side of the road. We Americans drive on the right side—in both senses of the word. We also drive cars that have the right stuff, meaning cars powered by big-inch V-8 engines that snarl and growl at stoplights. And when the light turns green, those angry engines with pistons the size of coffee cans unleash a fury to the rear tires; a process that's become an American trademark. Not even the spiraling cost of gasoline can fully squelch such illicit behavior.

Joanna Young and her 2005 Magnum happened to be the subject of an overhaul, thanks to her husband Andrew, another of Her Majesty's transplanted royal subjects. In fact, it was Andrew's own project car, a 1968 Dodge Charger, that inspired the overhaul. Joanna was simply enamored with the Charger's brute power from its

Chip Foose wanted to give the Magnum a more aggressive look up front. The solution was found in the Dodge's sister model, Chrysler's 300C. The A-Team removed the Magnum's front fascia and grille, then replaced it with a clip from a donor 300C. The difference is obvious on Joanna's overhauled car.

supercharged 500-cubic-inch V-8 (what else?). "She is jealous of my new project," Andrew jokingly shared with the *Overhaulin'* crew before the heist.

Moreover, Jo, as Andrew affectionately calls his wife, often teased her husband about how the new Hemi Magnum could blow the doors off the old Charger. "I have heard her say many times that her car would fly if it was supercharged," added Andrew. That was enough to get the A-Team in gear, and their mission was to give the car its supercharger, in this case a compact Paxton

Joanna now has the magic touch, thanks to Magic Touch, every time she opens the doors to her Magnum. "X" marks the spot on the doors where the A-Team removed the original door handles to make way for Magic Touch's one-touch buttons.

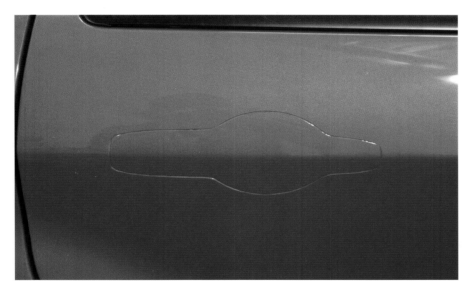

blower that easily fits under the Magnum's stock hood, or as they say in jolly England, "bonnet." Chip Foose had some other surprises in store for the car, too.

The heist required the assistance of Westoaks Chrysler-Dodge and the dealership's service writer, Jim Morrow, who easily gained Jo's trust when she dropped the car off for service. The dealership accommodated Jo with a loaner, a new Chrysler 300C, and as she drove home in the borrowed car, Chris Jacobs jumped in her car and headed straight for Keisler Compressors' shop for the seven-day makeover.

Filling the Magnum's stylish wheel wells was no problem for Chip Foose. He designed a set of five-spoke rims just for the car, then wrapped them with BFGoodrich's finest high-performance rubber.

Because the car was practically brand new, the deconstruction didn't require removing every nut and bolt. "A few things on this car we don't need to tear apart as we normally do," explained Craig Chaffers.

Among the first items the Yanks yanked off the body were the glue-on

The answer is blowing in the wind with the Vortec supercharger that the A-Team bolted onto the intake side of Joanna's Hemi V-8. The additional boost increases the car's performance substantially without compromising its tractability or reliability.

badges and emblems that littered the sheet metal. The warm blast from a standard handheld hair dryer made quick work of them; next the A-Team gutted the interior. Said Chip, "This is a new car, but we'll put a new interior in it." That task was left to Miles from Katzkin Interiors, and while he tackled that assignment, Chip made sketches to determine paint color, graphics, wheel sizes, and other modifications that would set this Magnum apart from all others on the road. This car was going to receive more than just the right stuff. It was destined to have the *Overhaulin'* stuff.

That's when Chip had a stroke of genius, deciding to substitute the front fascia from a Chrysler 300C for the Magnum's. He reasoned that the

Flame-and-graphic artist Mike Lavellee worked wonders on the car's graphics, but he also took his pyrotechnic act under the hood where he applied similar art work to the Hemi engine's air plenum.

Chrysler's grille and front bumper offered a more pronounced look, one that would give the Dodge a more aggressive appearance. Jim from the dealership located a customer willing to swap front ends, and the deal was consummated in the Keisler shop. Halfway through the swap Andrew saw the stripped-down Dodge and said, "In Foose we trust," and bit his lip hoping that the 300C's fascia would look good on his wife's car. In the words of co-host A. J., this was the "great Chrysler face off."

While new Eibach suspension was set in place to lower the car nearly two inches, Chris and Jim shifted into prank mode to play with Jo's mind and patience, telling her that the work to her car would take a little

longer than originally expected. She maintained a stiff upper lip and carried on while the A-Team ferried her car to Lanzini Body Works for its striking metallic orange/bronze base coat before Chip laid out the panels that would form the basis for the car's signature graphics—life-like fire by the master of flames, Mike Lavallee.

Chip wanted the flames to appear as though they were emerging from openings in the hood. To emphasize the three-dimensional graphics, Mike Lavellee painted the flame licks so they spilled onto the paint job itself.

Part of the overhaul includes presenting the mark with a complete artist's rendering by Chip Foose. These drawings reveal the car's bold lines even before the A-Team has a chance to finish the project.

"He's the king of fire," stated Chip. Then Mike set about to complete his pyrotechnic display on the car's hood, trunk lid, and engine intake plenum.

Watching Mike work the airbrush was a lesson in itself, and with each pass of the handheld gun, another lick of flame magically appeared over the show-quality paint job that Lanzini and crew had applied.

The flame burned bright for another prank by Chris and Jim, too. This time Jo was summoned to the dealership to pick up her car. While she waited at the service department's front door, another customer's truck—driven by Chris wearing a Westoaks dealership uniform—accelerated quickly through the parking lot, leaving more than a few shards of rubber in his wake. "You going to do that to my car?" Jo squeamishly asked Jim. No, but as it turned out, not even Jo was going to drive her Magnum that day, and she went home without her car.

By the seventh day the project was nearing completion. Joe and Geoff of J&G Audio, working with Sandy from Boston Acoustics, had the sound system wired and ready, Scott from GS Motors fine-tuned the Paxton supercharger, and O'Reilly Auto Parts donated a batch of accessories that would make life for Jo and her new car much easier. Car covers, cleaning products, roadside emergency items, and such

amounted to the O'Reilly Factor for this overhaul.

All that remained was the final prank and the reveal. For that Jo was called back to the dealership where she was told that one of the service mechanics had crashed her car. Apparently a baby bottle that Jo had left in the car slid under the brake pedal, resulting in a crash. The injured worker—played by none other than Chris Jacobs wearing a neck brace—was seeking restitution from the car's owner. Jim explained to Jo that since the accident occurred off the dealership's premises and the malfunction was due to negligence on her part, she was liable for damages. Jo was stunned and speechless.

At that time Chip appeared on the set to tell her, "Jo, you've been overhauled."

Jo was quite speechless during the car's reveal, too, and after a quick walk around she excitedly exclaimed, "I want to get in." Noticing there were no door handles, she asked, "How do you open it?" The crew from Magic Touch came out to show her how the nearly invisible push-button mechanisms worked, and all that remained was for her to drive the Magnum with its supercharged Hemi V-8. As she drove off into the sunset (which never happens in the British Empire), she proclaimed, "Andy, you're not touching it . . . ever!" Bloody rotten thanks a bloke gets for helping his mate!

'67 PONTIAC GTO
Sharon Sexton

Sharon and Geoff Sexton

A family is more than just a group of people sharing the same house. A family is a unit, a single entity that has a bond stronger than time and distance. Sharon and Geoff's family includes their two sons—and the 1967 Pontiac GTO. Moreover, Sharon's grandfather was a car guy, one who treated Sharon's car like family, always making sure the Pontiac was in top shape. When he passed away in the early 1990s, a part of the Pontiac seemed to die with him. Years later, with Geoff's help—and the A-Team's hard work—new life was pumped into the old Goat, and the family, it seemed, was again complete. The family grew in another way, too: Sharon and her brood are now part of the A-Team family. As Chris said at the end of the episode, "We're all family on the A-Team." And, as every mom knows, families stick together.

A mom is the cornerstone of her family. She's the chief cook and head bottle washer, banker and money manager, doctor and nurse, homework monitor and Sunday school teacher. She's the family taxi driver who attends all the soccer games and dance lessons, and the housekeeper and laundry maid making sure the castle is fit for the king.

But moms are not supposed to be knowledgeable about automobiles—especially fast cars like Pontiac's GTO, which is considered by experts to be the model that started the muscle car movement in the 1960s. So when Chip Foose and the A-Team selected Sharon Sexton for their next mark, they were up against one tough cookie maker. Sharon was what could best be described as a "car gal," because she knew from the get-go that her GTO was one fast customer. Her 1967 GTO also happened to be her very first car, which she bought in 1979 when she was 19 years old. She spent a lot of time behind the Goat's steering wheel, especially at the drag strip where

The thing that stood out most during the deconstruction phase was the rust buildup on the trunk's floor pan, prompting one A-Team member to comment, "Want a piece of the floor?"

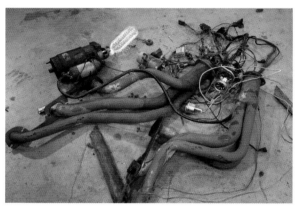

Old car parts never die, they just fade away. Like entrails of a dead animal, the Goat's exhaust headers and miscellaneous parts lie strewn on the garage floor at Kaeser Compressors.

she won more than a fair share of races. She never sold the car, either, and the old Goat later served as her four-wheel delivery wagon: "This is the car I drove my first born home from the hospital in," she would tell the A-Team at the GTO's reveal.

Those moments of quiet reminiscing would have to wait, though, because Sharon was about to get overhauled. She had her husband to thank for the week of stress and uncertainty that awaited her, too. The episode began innocently enough as husband Geoff, acting as the insider, made sure that the long Pontiac's rear bumper stuck out a little too far onto the public sidewalk in front of their house, creating the perfect scenario for an alleged complaint from a neighbor. Then, as Sharon assumed her taxi driver role to run an errand in the family car, leaving the GTO alone at the homestead,

In its prime, the classic V-8 engine saw a lot of action at the drag strip during what Sharon's husband termed "her wilder days." Sharon's grandfather kept the engine in tip-top tune.

the A-Team jumped into action when Chris Jacobs and Joel from Carr Towing plucked the car from the driveway. They drove straight to Kaeser Compressors for its overhaul.

The GTO's deconstruction led to several revelations about the aging car, among them a rusted-out trunk pan and misaligned trunk-lid hinges due to a rear-end crash. It was also time to prank Sharon. A. J. phoned her to leave a prerecorded message from the so-called "Orange County Impound Department" describing their hours of operation. The message was purposely confusing to fluster Sharon. She kept her cool, however, so Chris took over with a follow-up call, posing as Keith Baker from the county impound yard. He reassured Sharon that she could pick up the car once the paperwork was completed. This was followed by another call from A. J.—acting as Bridgette from the yard—informing Sharon about the accrued fees and what documents she'd need to present

Full-on restorations often take months—even years—to complete. The A-Team had the GTO's body stripped within a day, and before the end of the week it was reassembled and ready for the road.

The scars of a fender-bender were exposed when the Pontiac's paint was stripped. The damaged section required additional attention from the team. Meanwhile, Andreas Somogyi repaired the rusted trunk pan.

before the car could be released back to her. Little did our mark know she was being set up for an even bigger prank later at the impound yard.

As for the overhaul, things were going rather smoothly. The body had been stripped of paint and most of the metalwork was finished enough so that Pete Santini's crew could complete the final prep for paint, an R-M mix that Chip dubbed Midnight Blue. Then the rain

Chip Foose selected a paint color he termed Midnight Blue. After the Santini team applied the paint, Dennis Rickliffs took over to lay down the stripe job that accented the car's dark color.

Victor and the Intro Wheels crew put their CNC machines to work to cut and polish the five-spoke wheels. The Foose-designed wheels are wrapped with BFGoodrich rubber and are awaiting mounting.

came down, forcing everybody and the Goat back to Chip's shop, where the paint was applied and the body set in the temperature-controlled booth to bake dry.

Sharon's parade was rained on, too, when she showed up at the impound yard to retrieve her GTO. The yard manager, played by Martin, threw one obstacle after another Sharon's way until the total impound fee came to $1,975. Sharon was prepared to write a check—all she

wanted was her GTO back—when Martin told her he couldn't release the car unless she had all the proper forms filled out. Then he dropped the bombshell on her: He offered her $50 for the car, in essence saving her nearly $2,000. After all, he reminded her, the car was *old*. That pretty much got her goat, and Sharon eventually left the impound yard in a huff, and without her car.

It was time for the reveal. The A-Team was putting the finishing

The dash insert, center console, and steering wheel look like they're made of wood, right? They're not. Chip Foose used an old trick—requiring a blow torch—for the wood-grain appearance. Bill Dunn stitched the upholstery.

Butler Performance slipped in a brand-new crate engine for the overhaul. The 461-cubic-inch V-8 developed 475 horsepower on the dyno. "I think that's gonna get the job done," said Chris Jacobs.

touches on the GTO, attaching the Hotchkis suspension components and Baer brakes to the underside, and making sure the 475-horsepower Butler Performance engine and Bowler transmission were working properly. As Chris and A. J. were running out of pranks to pull on Sharon, she was running out of patience. There was, however, one more prank to pull, and this time Chris and Martin played the good cop–bad cop routine on her. Naturally, Martin was the bad cop, again pressuring Sharon when she showed up at the impound yard for her car. If looks could kill, Sharon's stare would have put Martin six feet under. He was saved when Chris— aka Keith Baker—showed up. A

The GTO was among the hottest-performing muscle cars of the 1960s. This is a familiar sight that many other drivers were treated to "back in the day" of muscle cars.

shouting match pursued until the yard's owner, played by Chip Foose, came out of the office to settle the matter, finally revealing to Sharon that she—more specifically, her 1967 Pontiac GTO—had been overhauled.

In the end the A-Team made sure this was the mother of all overhauls. After all, they did it for Sharon, mother of two, and one mom who certainly knows her cars.

'69 FIREBIRD CONVERTIBLE
Dennis Kahn

Dennis is joined by his girlfriend Stephanie Arculli—also the episode's insider—in front of his overhauled 1969 Firebird and the A-Team at the conclusion of the reveal. For the past few years, Dennis wanted to restore the classy convertible, but time and money were always in short supply—until the A-Team stepped in to help at Stephanie's request. Chalk up one more successful overhaul to the *Overhaulin'* A-Team.

Dennis and Stephanie

It was a beautiful day in the neighborhood for Dennis Kahn when he left his 1969 Pontiac Firebird convertible parked in front of his home. But the beautiful day turned into an ugly week of frustration and anger for Dennis after Chris Jacobs drove away in his car. Dennis had been marked for an overhaul by his girlfriend, Stephanie Arculli, and it was Chris' job to heist the Firebird for delivery to *Hot Rod* and *Car Craft Magazine's* shop in nearby Los Angeles where the A-Team awaited. As Chris drove off into the night, he said for the *Overhaulin'* camera's benefit: "If you [Dennis] love this car so much, why'd you leave it unlocked, man?" Roger that, Chris.

With the convertible secured in the *Hot Rod/Car Craft* garage, the A-Team readied the car for its overhaul. That meant, of course, disassembly—or in *Overhaulin'* vernacular: the deconstruction phase. As the parts were removed, the A-Team was greeted by large sections of rust in the car's sheet metal. Then more rust. And yet more rust after that.

Ripped and torn upholstery greeted the A-Team during the deconstruction phase, so the interior was stripped clean, leaving room for Bill Dunn's team to trim the seats, dashboard, and floor.

Among the personal items recovered from the car was a pair of old binoculars, prompting Chris to joke, "Looks like Dennis has been on the lookout for a new car." Then an A-Team member exposed even more rust in the old Pontiac's body panels, and Chris shrugged, adding, "Even the binoculars are rusted." Clearly, a lot of metal work would be required to get this old rust bucket looking good for the next neighborhood block party. Fortunately, the good neighbors at Year One offered enough replacement parts to help make the car look new again.

By Day 2, the car had been stripped clean, and A-Team members were cutting, welding, grinding, and hammering away at its sheet metal. An optimistic Shawn Hengstebeck commented on the team's progress, "We're looking pretty good." Countered Craig Chaffers, "There's a lot of rust repair. It's all about the rust."

Rust or no rust, the A-Team wasn't going to let Dennis rest easy, hoping that the local police department would recover his car. It was time to toy with the mark's mind. Plan A was to send team member Bryant to Dennis' house to talk about the missing car and invite him to join the Neighborhood Watch program. Dennis listened tentatively as Bryant explained the goals of the program and the obligations of its members. Dennis signed up and was given his "official" Neighborhood

By the end of Day 1, the A-Team had the Firebird stripped and ready for media blasting. They rolled the car out of the Hot Rod/Car Craft *shop to strip away all the old paint and Bondo.*

Watch sign and cap, and then Bryant asked him to recite the Neighborhood Watch pledge. Standing a few feet away was Chris, dressed as a bagman wandering the streets. He, too, raised his right hand and mumbled his version of the Neighborhood Watch pledge. Dennis would encounter the vagabond again before the overhaul was finished.

Back at the shop, Chip Foose's watch told him it was time to make a few sketches of what Dennis' car *should* look like. He sketched three variations, each one a different color.

A lot of metal work was required to prepare the body for paint. The A-Team asked a special favor from West Coast Customs for the paint job.

But it was the fourth rendering, one in blue, that Stephanie said would suit Dennis the most. With the body ready for paint, the A-Team invited the crew from West Coast Customs to apply the R-M paint. They dubbed the color Foose Fade because they were

With only hours to go before the reveal, the A-Team encountered a few minor problems with the drivetrain. But once the 400-cubic-inch engine, rebuilt by L&R Automotive, fired up, the job was finished.

It's always a frenzy of work during the final hours. Like a swarm of locusts, the A-Team attacks the Firebird one final time to make sure everything works properly for the mark, Dennis Kahn.

going to blend the blue shade to a lighter hue below the body's beltline.

Ryan Friedlinghaus, owner of West Coast Customs, had his entire crew on the job. At one point, two members of the West Coast Customs team brought an aquarium into the shop, placing it—with Chip's

blessing—in the backseat area. Everyone had a few chuckles, then Chip got serious, "Now get that thing out of here!" It was back to business, and in no time the WCC boys had the car's sheet metal sealed with primer, then ready for paint. By sunrise the next morning the Pontiac had been painted and rubbed out.

Later Ryan shared that "working with *Overhaulin'* gives us a chance to show the world what we really want to show them." In short, this was a quality real-world paint job, one that any car owner would be proud to have on his or her ride. No doubt, Dennis was going to be surprised—and pleased.

He'd find a nice surprise under the Firebird's curvaceous hood, too.

Overhaulin' and West Coast Custums— joined forces to rebuild this 1969 Firebird convertible. The gang from West Coast Customs applied the paint.

The guys at L&R Automotive rebuilt the 400-cubic-inch engine, dressing it with fine high-performance jewelry from Summit Racing. Then the oil level was topped with Royal Purple's finest chemically engineered synthetic lubricant. A Keisler Engineering five-speed automatic transmission with overdrive was spliced into the drivetrain, and the chassis was kissed with Hotchkis underpinnings and Baer brakes.

It's all about the ride, and to improve the ride the overhauled Firebird rides on a set of Avalon wheels with BFGoodrich rubber. The suspension is from Hotchkis, and Baer disc brakes are at all four corners.

All that was left to do was take Dennis for another ride, so to speak, with the final prank. For that, Dennis was treated with the return of the bagman, Lazio, played by Chris. This time Chris, er, Lazio, approached Dennis in front of his home, telling him that he knew where his car was,

and that a "team" had been watching the block every day. Dennis didn't catch the "team" reference, and quizzed Lazio more, almost forcing him into a corner until, finally, the Overhaulin' camera crew approached from the rear, revealing the prank. Lazio transformed into

L&R Automotive rebuilt the 400-cubic-inch engine, using parts from Summit Racing's vast inventory. Keisler Engineering installed the five-speed overdrive automatic transmission, and Royal Purple oil serves as the engine's lifeblood.

Chris Jacobs, and Dennis melded back into his usual happy-go-lucky self. And his car—his overhauled car—was ready for him. Well, nearly ready, because the A-Team encountered a few minor obstacles that forced them to seat Dennis in the nearby film-crew trailer for about an hour while the car received its finishing touches.

When it was time to escort Dennis into the shop, a totally different car greeted him, and, after a few expletives that the FCC censors bleeped out, he surveyed the car closely. Chris sidled up to him and said casually, "No rust."

Replied Dennis, "Yeah, no rust." Dennis had his car back, and the Neighborhood Watch had one more member on its team of watchdogs. No doubt, it was, once again, a beautiful day in the neighborhood. Roger, over and out.

OVERLORD

D-Day takes on new meaning at Overhaulin'

There was nothing simple about Episode 326, known as Overlord. The marked truck was a 1956 Ford F-100, among the most desirable pickup trucks for customizing, and the marked man was what *Overhaulin'* show producer Bud Brutsman describes as "the best car designer in the world." That would be Chip Foose.

"In the four and a half years I've known Chip Foose," said Brutsman, "he's never done anything for himself." All of Chip's time and energy put into the TV program has been for the Marks and their families. Throughout, Chip's '56 Ford sat forlornly in the Foose Design parking lot getting rustier, dustier, and crustier by the day.

Brutsman decided to change that, after Foose's long-time friend Gary Fulkerson pitched him the concept of overhauling Foose. Brutsman gathered the best A-Team he could, enlisting Chip's father, Sam Foose, to head the overhaul. One night they "stole" the truck, and as a diversion they removed the "Foose Design" sign from the outside wall.

Chip called his dad immediately after he learned of the heist. "When I heard my dad's voice crack, I started to think it [the theft] was for real," said Chip. Overlord was underway, but the hard part was yet to come. How would they overhaul the truck belonging to one of the most demanding—in terms of style and execution—car builders in the world?

The answer was found in the rough sketches that Chip had made of his truck a few years before. Reviewing the drawings, Sam knew exactly what his son had in mind. The A-Team went to work, altering the truck's sheet metal ever so slightly,

making it hard to pinpoint the exact modifications. It's customizing according to the Chip Foose doctrine, and for the next few months it would be played out by Sam, Craig Chaffers, Charlie Hutton, Andreas Somogyi, and many others who had worked side by side with Chip on past *Overhaulin'* episodes.

"You're building a car for a guy who is the greatest car designer on the planet," Brutsman reminded the crew. Challenged like never before, the A-Team proceeded with the plan until, about six months later working as stealthily as possible, the truck was ready for its reveal at the SEMA Show in Las Vegas where Chip was a celebrity guest.

Chris Jacobs escorted Chip to the Roush Racing booth where he was scheduled to assist Jack Roush in presenting a new crate engine to the market. That was the ploy, and Chip cut the ribbon. When he snipped the scissors, the curtain behind him rose, unveiling his finished truck. Initially Chip wasn't aware of the situation until he noticed all eyes were directed behind him. Curious, he turned to see his truck for the first time in months. "This is mine?" he stuttered. The man who had been in the cat-bird seat for so many pranks had been pranked

It was an emotional moment, but Chip's words best described his feelings when he said, "The number one thing about this build was that my dad was involved." Fittingly, Chip's plans are to pass the old shop truck on to his son, Brock, when he's old enough to drive.

But the episode known as Overlord wasn't complete until the whole world heard the words: "My name is Chip, and I've just been overhauled!"

INDEX